By the Same Author

★

TWENTIETH CENTURY DRAWINGS
NICHOLAS HILLIARD AND ISAAC OLIVER
(Victoria and Albert Museum Handbook, 1947)

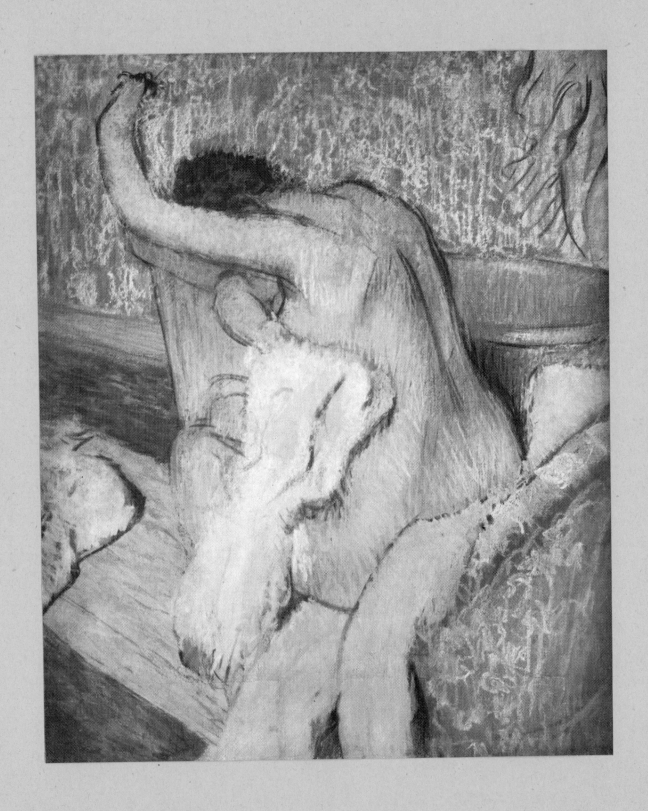

DEGAS: Après le bain

NINETEENTH CENTURY DRAWINGS

1850-1900

by

GRAHAM REYNOLDS

Deputy Keeper, Victoria and Albert Museum

LONDON : PLEIADES BOOKS : MCMXLIX

First published 1949 *by*
PLEIADES BOOKS LTD 11 FITZROY SQUARE LONDON W1
Printed in Great Britain by
THE SHENVAL PRESS LONDON AND HERTFORD

ACKNOWLEDGMENTS

★

THE author's grateful thanks are due to the owners of drawings whose permission to reproduce them is separately acknowledged in the List of Plates; also to those who have helped him with advice, by making photographs available or in other ways; in particular, Sir Kenneth Clark, K.C.B., Dr P. A. Rave of Berlin, Dr Grete Ring and Sir Robert Witt, C.B.E.; and to Messrs. J. M. Dent and Sons Ltd. for permission to make use of the extracts from R. Muther's *History of Modern Painting* (1907 edition) quoted on pages 42 and 47.

CONTENTS

*

ILLUSTRATIONS

★

ILLUSTRATIONS

9

NINETEENTH CENTURY DRAWINGS

ILLUSTRATIONS

11

NINETEENTH CENTURY DRAWINGS

ILLUSTRATIONS IN THE TEXT

Introduction

*

AT first sight there seems little scope for generalizing about the art of the
second half of the nineteenth century. We are accustomed to think in terms
of the painting of the period, and to assess that painting almost entirely by
the achievements of the French Impressionists, with perhaps a wistful
glance at the Pre-Raphaelites in England; therefore a great amount of excellent work
which is not comprised under those heads goes disregarded. It is of course incontestable
that the greatest vitality within the period was displayed by the Impressionist artists,
but many who were not Impressionists found it possible to work, without distorting
their intentions, in a more traditional idiom. It is probably easier to estimate the contribution of these less spectacular figures in the years 1850—1900, and thereby to re-
assert the continuity and comparative homogeneity of the Western European tradition,
by studying the drawings rather than the paintings of this period. For one reason, such
a survey brings in artists who would otherwise remain unconsidered, such as Redon,
Steinlen, Beardsley, Keene, and Rodin. For another, drawing before 1900 was less
divorced than painting from its former history. The painters had been studying the
scientists, and applying new ideas on light to their palettes and techniques; but, in spite
of the influence of the Japanese print, design had not yet been subject to a correspondingly disruptive analysis—it was due to receive it at the hands of Picasso and Braque in
the first decade of the twentieth century.

Admittedly, art was advancing on an uneven front in France, England and Germany
in the years under review in this book, but that was no novelty. When the Renaissance
began to spread through Western Europe from Italy in the fifteenth century it thawed
the Netherlands, France and Germany at very different rates and with varying degrees
of effectiveness, whilst England was left to shiver in Gothic isolation till the closing
years of the sixteenth century. Again, if there was ever a time when we should have
expected one universal art language to be current in Europe we should look for it in the
eighteenth century; and yet whose styles could be more divergent than those of the contemporary Greuze and Reynolds, Tiepolo and Mengs? That there is as wide a difference
between the styles of Renoir and Alfred Stevens, Leibl and the later Van Gogh is not in
itself a reason for ignoring either party to the comparison.

As they lived through the second half of the nineteenth century the protagonists of

13

the national schools remained conveniently unaware of the latest developments in neighbouring countries. When Pissarro and Monet were exiled in England from the Franco-Prussian war the land of Constable and Turner saw no merit in their pictures. The taste for foreign art was in fact a generation in arrears; Impressionism took root in Germany and England in the 'nineties, when it was being superseded by post-Impressionism in France, and the English painters whose absence from the Salon of 1859 was regretted by Baudelaire included Leslie, Hook, Maclise and Martin—characteristic figures of the Early Victorian age.

Granting this time lag in appreciation, Europe remained a geographical unity, in which a surprising number of fruitful international contacts were made between artists. Rome retained its centuries-old attraction; to it came Degas and Renoir from France, Stevens and Leighton from England, Feuerbach and von Marées from Germany. Paris was beginning to contest the primacy of Rome as an artists' centre: Menzel and Leibl, Poynter, Leighton, Whistler and many others came to it for training in art. Leighton's itinerary as a student is indeed a model of cosmopolitanism, and a good index to the eclecticism of the academic artist of his time, for he studied in Rome, Florence, Brussels and Paris, and most fruitfully of all in Frankfurt. The positive fruits of the interchange of ideas between national schools are instanced by the imprint left by the study of Cornelius, Rethel and Schorr von Carolsfeld on Tenniel, Sandys and other illustrators of the 'sixties, and by the fact that Degas made a copy of Menzel's glittering painting of Potsdam court life, 'The Ball Room'.

When the field of study is restricted to the Impressionists their choice of contemporary life as the subject matter of their art becomes the paramount feature of the period; but by holding the scales more evenly we attain to a broader view of the European scene in the years from 1850 to 1900. Certainly in France so intransigent a challenge to the traditions of historical painting and the grand manner was sensational; but in England no such violent reaction was called for. A succession of painters—for instance, Highmore, Zoffany, Wilkie, Mulready, Webster—had carried on the tradition of contemporary actuality from Hogarth's time down to the middle of the nineteenth century. In Germany Menzel was able to paint a reception at court or the scene in an iron works without self-consciously breaking new ground or committing unheard-of assaults on contemporary taste.

The decisive trends in England and Germany were, then, continuations of those current in the first half of the century. Romanticism, under its twin aspects of love of the distant in space and time, entered upon a new phase with the archaic medievalism of the Pre-Raphaelites; and at the same time it joined forces with Classicism to produce the Grecian and Roman histories and idylls of Leighton, Poynter, Moore, Feuerbach, Böcklin and von Marées. By the side of this Romantic and Classical-Romantic art went the work of the illustrators, who never drew better than when they dealt with the life of their own times.

In making the selection of drawings which is discussed and reproduced in the following pages I have been mindful of the dictum of Samuel Butler that 'hard-and-fast lines ever cut the fingers of those who draw them'. Interpreted in one way my subject could include any drawings executed between the years 1850 and 1900—for instance, the latest works of Delacroix and Mulready or the earliest works of Shannon and Ricketts. Interpreted in another it would show only the work of those born (say) between 1830 and 1880 who came to artistic maturity in the years in question. I have not applied either of these principles with rigid logic, but I have sought in my choice, while limiting it to drawings which I believe to have been made in the second half of the nineteenth century, to underline the characteristic pattern of the period. Delacroix and Mulready seem to me to belong to the first half of the century; Guys, though born in 1805, to the second, and I think Daumier belongs as much to the second half of the century as to the first. That there are many omissions both of artists and of drawings I am fully aware; some are due to limitation of space, some to the persisting difficulties of tracing and photographing collections, particularly abroad, in the immediate post-war period, some to my defects of knowledge, some to my personal predilections. In particular I have severely limited the representation of the English illustrators, whose work is so closely allied to the reproduction for wood-engraving for which it was designed that it requires separate treatment. But I think the choice presented gives a coherent and truthful impression of a period which though it is still near our own times may already be viewed with some approach to historical perspective. It is manifest that though the primacy of the French school cannot be disputed, great and vital drawings were produced in England and Germany in this half-century.

The French School

*

THE clash of two diametrically opposed artistic theories in France in the middle of the nineteenth century is summed up by Daumier in a well-known lithograph in which he shows Ingres tilting at Delacroix in front of the *Institut de France*. Delacroix bears the slogan 'Line is Colour' and Ingres carries a shield inscribed 'Colour is Utopia, Long live line'. It was indeed in the sphere of colour that the most violent revolution of the century was to take place, and the vigour and éclat of the Impressionists is demonstrated as much in the brilliant palette they brought to their paintings as in the actuality of their subject matter. A corresponding impetus to novelty in design was given by the Japanese prints which became increasingly popular and influential after their chance discovery by the engraver Bracquemond in 1856. But with this impulse toward novelty and the resolve to inquire into new possibilities of development at any price, went, so far as drawing is concerned, a strong undercurrent of traditionalism. In the drawings of the second half of the nineteenth century it is Ingres with his 'Drawing is the probity of art', and not Delacroix with the momentum of his tensely coiled line, who is the more powerful influence. Of the artists illustrated in the plates which follow we can really only instance Daumier, Cézanne, Steinlen and Forain as in any way preserving the vigorous baroque handwriting of Delacroix.

The traditional manner of drawing as taught in the studios was then a substantial formative influence not only upon the academic artists but also in the drawings of, for instance, Degas and Renoir, Seurat and Van Gogh. The studio of Gleyre may be taken as representative of the methods of training in use, and has the historic importance of having been frequented by Renoir, Monet, Sisley and Bazille as well as Poynter, Whistler and Du Maurier. From the description of Carrel's studio in *Trilby* ('Carrel' is a pseudonym for Gleyre) we learn that the students drew or painted every weekday on alternate weeks from the nude male or female model, and that on Fridays Gleyre came round to spend a few minutes at each drawing board or easel. Gleyre himself, after a voyage to the Near East which was quite in keeping with the Byronic spirit prevalent in his youth, had developed a not unpleasing mode of painting scenes of the classical age which is more nearly reflected in the work of Poynter than in any of the other students we have mentioned. He had inherited his studio from Delaroche, and, remembering his own financial struggles as a student, ran it on a co-operative basis and not for profit.

The place that drawing the female figure had in the art world of which Gleyre was by no means a despicable member is well illustrated by an episode witnessed by his friend and biographer, Clément. A girl came to the artist's apartments; she was badly in need of money, and asked if she could pose for him. Dressed as she was in poor and ragged clothing she was of a most unpromising appearance. Gleyre said that he did not need a model. The girl insisted, importuned him. 'All right,' he said, 'take off your clothes and I'll see.' He resumed his conversation with his friend. When he remembered the girl and turned back to look at her he stopped short in amazement; then his eyes filled with tears as he contemplated the perfection of her form. 'Il dévorait des yeux cette superbe créature. . . . Il se détourna pour cacher son émotion,' says Clément. It is equally characteristic of this academic world that, after his outburst of emotion, Gleyre should, in painting the girl, have improved upon details of her form from another model, and then placed the whole in an Empire *mise-en-scène* with the title 'Sappho'. But his original lyrical feeling was not far from Renoir's appreciation of the opulence of the female body, its *tétons* and *fesses*.

In opposition to this traditional method of tuition Lecoq de Boisbaudran advocated a system of his own invention designed especially to train the artistic memory. In essentials this consisted of making the drawing from memory when the original was no longer in front of the eyes. Fantin-Latour, Legros, Rodin and Dalou were pupils of Lecoq de Boisbaudran, and his methods, learned at second-hand, influenced Whistler. His most original idea was to take his pupils into woods in which the models were walking about freely and unclothed. Thus relieved of the stilted restraint of their classroom postures, they moved naturally into graceful poses, which they would be asked to hold while the students memorized or sketched them. Rodin brought this method to full fruition in causing his models to roam about his studio at the Hotel Byron and its grounds.

The copying of other drawings was a supplement to, or substitute for, life drawing. Charles Bargue was especially reputed for his clever lithographic copies of drawings by his contemporaries Gérôme, Gleyre, Flandrin and the like, which he made into a home course of drawing, beginning with outline studies and ending with copies of the old masters. The loan of this 'Cours de Dessin Bargue' was an important event to Van Gogh in 1880 when he was seeking to invigorate his 'draughtsman's fist'. Indeed he was so intent on following its precepts that when he came to the copies after Old Masters prescribed in the course he had to move out of his constricted hovel in search of more elbow room.

Of the Old Masters whose drawings were prescribed for emulation and imitation none were held higher in regard than the portrait drawings of Holbein. They are the culminating point of Bargue's 'Cours de Dessin', they were set by Lecoq de Boisbaudran as memory exercises for his pupils, and copies of Holbein's drawings are found in the work of Degas and Seurat. The characteristics of Holbein's style are a nice combination of sensitivity and precision in the contour, linked to profound psychological subtlety;

they are clearly more closely akin to the outlook of Ingres than that of Delacroix. Of Holbein's nineteenth-century disciples Degas entered fully into that heritage, whilst Legros, who tried harder and more literally to do so, failed in the attempt.

Baudelaire, with his habitual critical acumen, resolved the deadlock between the adherents of Ingres and of Delacroix by maintaining that there is a drawing of line, and a drawing of colour and movement; Ingres is the great exponent of the former, Delacroix of the latter style. He added that Daumier was a draughtsman as gifted as either of these protagonists—a judgment which seemed a paradox when it was made, for journalistic draughtsmen were then despised. Baudelaire's judgment is a commonplace now; the consummate series of lithographs which Daumier poured out between 1830 and 1872 contains ample evidence of his greatness of mind. This series of over 3,500 works comprises a graphic *Comédie Humaine* which seems to leave no aspect of bourgeois life untouched. It has its roots in the unrestrained English caricature of the late eighteenth and early nineteenth century, but the graphic style has little in common with the timid lithographs by HB (John Doyle) which are presumed to have induced Philipon to found the paper *La Caricature*, in which Daumier's first noteworthy work appears. His style is constantly developing, the line becoming more cursive, the outline which makes for ever ridiculous the face it circumscribes always becoming more cruel and masterful.

His lithographic materials favoured a broad free line with velvety blacks and many nuances. As if in deliberate contrast Daumier used a fine pen outline in his drawings properly so-called; but the breadth of the lighting remains, and the sculptural solidity of the individual figures recalls how he had drawn some of his earliest caricatures of political celebrities from masks he himself had modelled. In the subject matter of his drawings he prefers (and this is true also of his paintings) themes less palpably absurd than the subjects of his published caricatures. He had an aspiration toward the creation of a grand, monumental art which was not fully satisfied by his cartoons for the popular Press, although nowadays we may see in those ephemera the apex of his art. Nevertheless such a drawing as 'The mountebank' (Plate 1) is oppressive in its pathos through its restraint; the artist has not caricatured the weariness of the old woman seated on a box, or set out by any marked exaggerations to make the little troupe ridiculous, and the greater interest of other attractions for the crowd has needed no underlining. The energy of the pen outline is in striking contrast to the sombre tinting of wash, which accords so well with the air of listless despondency which seems to brood over the group in the foreground.

In similar images, often repeated as though he were striving to reach a definitive treatment of his vision, Daumier drew or painted a small cycle of subjects: Don Quixote; Collectors Examining Prints; the Third Class Railway Carriage. No one could better express the terrifying impression of a crowd in the process of being fused by the spark of rebellion, or flying in fear. In the main body of his work he had no successor, but in one phase of it, the mordant caricatures of the legal profession, he created a type which was developed yet farther in drawing by Forain and in painting by Rouault. The contrast between the inexorable power of the law and the personal pettiness of its exponents has been apparent to many minds, but Daumier was the first to give it graphic expression; lawyers were to him what priests were to Goya (Plate 2 bottom).

For a long time the taste of collectors of modern French art in this country fossilized round the works of the Barbizon school. The collections which they put together, especially in the 'eighties and 'nineties, favoured the works of Corot, Rousseau, Daubigny and Millet; less fortunate than America, we were late to appreciate the riches of Impressionism. By a natural reaction there is now a tendency to undervalue the Barbizon painters. They are treated with the worst injustice of which criticism is capable: that of being regarded merely as forerunners of something greater, without proper regard to their own merits. When the time has come for them to be valued again in their own right it will be clear that they did what they set out to do—in Rousseau's words 'the objects represented are not there solely as they are, but . . . contain under a natural appearance the sentiments which they have stirred in our souls'.

The most forceful draughtsman of the Barbizon school was Millet; and to many who admire his work his drawings are more acceptable than his paintings with their crude and muddy tonalities. Himself a peasant, he was the first artist since the Dutch painters of the seventeenth century to express the life of the peasant as it really is, stripped of the false glamour of the shepherds and shepherdesses in Marie Antoinette's *hameau*, or the good-humoured frolics of the genre piece. Once the authentic simplicity of his treatment had been appreciated it gave rise to a whole series of similar expositions—by Israels in Holland, Segantini in Italy, the early Liebermann in Germany. Millet was consistently admired by Van Gogh who, at the very beginning of his artistic career, and again in the last months of his life, copied the wood-engravings after his 'Les Quatres Heures du Jour'. Indeed, it remained Van Gogh's unresolved ambition to paint like Millet a picture of a 'Sower' in which the figure of a man should appear as a universal symbol of humanity.

The prevailing tone of Millet's reading of the breaking hardships of peasant life is sufficiently well translated in the once world-famous poem 'The Man with the Hoe' which Edwin Markham wrote after seeing one of his pictures:

> *Bowed by the weight of centuries he leans*
> *Upon his hoe and gazes on the ground,*
> *The emptiness of ages in his face.*

Millet's peasants are generally impersonal symbols because a life of subjection to the soil leaves little room for the variations of individual character, and with his horror of uselessness and mere padding out of space he was not disposed to burke this fact. But the drawing of a shepherdess (Plate 4) was made in one of his more tender and indulgent moods. In this solid and satisfying drawing of a young girl leaning against a tree in the sunlight he has made no more concessions to conventional standards of physical beauty than has Degas in his studies of the 'petits rats' of the ballet; but the quaintness and charm of youth is all the more movingly portrayed because such comforting illusions are absent.

19

Boudin also is a precursor of the Impressionists; it was he who saw the talent in the juvenile caricatures of Claude Monet and urged him to take up painting in the open air. In spite of pressure from the more realistically-minded of his younger disciples he refused to leave out the gaily dressed, brightly coloured crinolined groups which are the chief charm of his scenes of Deauville and Trouville: 'They are there, why should I not paint them?' was his attitude. Although Proust modelled his painter Elstir as a composite sort of Impressionist, largely with the traits of Monet, it is the memory of a Boudin that the 'Seascape, with Frieze of Girls' most nearly evokes. Boudin is in the great tradition of sea painters, the heir of the sea-pieces by the Van de Velde and of Constable's brilliant oil sketches of Brighton. When however we compare his light and flickering sketches (Plate 3 top) with our nearest equivalent—for instance, *Rhyl Sands* by David Cox—we can see the difference between the wild but rather strained romanticism of the English artist and Boudin's preoccupation with the broad and gay visual characteristics of the scene, harmonized with his purely French feeling for social elegance.

Manet is in the anomalous position of being an Impressionist who never exhibited at any of the exhibitions which gave the group its name, and a reluctant leader of the *avant garde*, whose heart was set upon tradition and the Old Masters. With the exception of the pastels to which he turned in the last years of his life, drawing does not play a large part in Manet's output. Primarily a colourist, he conforms well to Delacroix's description of that temperament 'The colourists, the men who unite all the phases of painting, have to establish, at once and from the beginning, everything that is proper and essential to their art. They have to mass things in with colour even as the sculptor does with clay, marble or stone; their sketch, like that of the sculptor, must also render proportion, perspective, effect and colour.' The scandal his paintings caused was due as much to their uncompromising breadth of brush-work and their vividness of colour as to the supposedly scabrous modernity of his subject matter. A public which was accustomed to the enamel-like finish of the followers of David could not stomach this appearance of the unfinished sketch.

In his comparatively rare drawings Manet shows the same summary rapidity and instinctive grasp of essentials to the exclusion of detail; more than any of his contemporaries he could approach to the brisk suggestive calligraphy of the Oriental races. But in his famous painting 'Olympia' Manet turned in memory to Titian's Venus of Urbino, of which he had made a copy during his early visit to Italy, and to the magnificent Maja Desnuda of Goya, whom he admired equally with the Spanish masters of the seventeenth century. The sanguine sketch (Plate 6) shows the deliberate care with which he built upon his models in spite of the apparent fluidity of his brush-work. Even the features of his favourite model, Victorine Meurend, are suppressed in his determination to fix the balance of light and shade and the firm pressure of the form upon the bed. It is hard, in looking at this unrevolutionary figure study, which might almost, but for its greater ability, have come from the studio of Flandrin or Gérôme, to conceive the horror which the painting evoked on its exhibition in 1865; but everything Manet did was suspect after he had shown a nude model in the company of two men in contemporary dress in 'Le Déjeuner sur l'Herbe'. 'Pertuiset the lion-hunter' (Plate 3 bottom) is of altogether freer handling. It marks the preliminary conception of the open-air portrait which, when exhibited at the Salon in 1881, gained Manet the official award of a medal and so made him at last independent of the suffrages of the jury. The sketch is of the most casual kind, the shading consists of swift and violent scribbling, and yet it crystallizes the painter's intentions in an individual and vivacious handwriting.

Degas said of himself that he was born to be a draughtsman, and his whole career as a painter revolved round the study and practice of drawing. He never forgot that Ingres had said to him 'Draw lines, young man, many lines, from memory or from nature; it is in this way that you will become a good artist.' The rigorous course of copying to which he devoted himself in the Louvre and in Italy reinforced this advice. His earlier drawings, such as the study for 'Les malheurs de la ville d'Orléans' (Plate 7) and Horsewoman (Plate 8), show to what good purpose he had put his admiration for Holbein and Ingres. The precision of outline, the colourful soft contour, and the immobility of the subjects, could not be in greater contrast to the brutally rough sketches of his later manner. Yet already a note of actuality is apparent, which portends that the draughtsman will not be for ever content with such history pieces as the 'Misfortunes of the town of Orléans'. Never an open-air painter, his link with the Impressionists came about through his desire to paint contemporary life, and through a restless curiosity and independence of spirit which made him seek constantly for new facets of perception. Above all he was preoccupied with the rendering of movement; he studied the gait of horses in sculptures of his own modelling and in Muybridge's successive instantaneous photographs as well as in his drawings. It is to this passion for the study of motion, and above all for motion combined with light, that we owe his great series of drawings and pastels of ballet dancers, laundresses and women bathing themselves.

Baudelaire had said that the painter should seek beauty in modern life, and in their various ways Manet, Renoir and Degas, no less than Guys, were intent upon that search. But while Renoir found a beauty that was lyrical and voluptuous, and Manet a beauty that was almost prettiness, Degas sought no seductive models or conventionally attractive scenes. He strips the ballet of all enchantments of sex, and shows the chorus and stars alike as they are, plain unglamorous girls, slaves as hard-working as Millet's peasants. Yet the enchantment remains in his paintings, as it does in the theatre itself even when the onlooker realizes that he is being deceived by shadows, trick lighting and grease-paint; the enchantment remains in the colour, in the light from the footlights which illumines the dancers as they are seen on the stage, and in the sheer act of intelligence and will with which Degas comprehends their bodies and summarizes them in swift stumpy strokes. It resides also in the solution he has found to the paradox in painting which perplexed him most—how to show in one aspect of a body, which must be still, that the body is in motion. For all the apparent crudity of outline in such drawings as Plate 22 no anatomical detail is shirked: the marvel is not only their compression and summary completeness but also all they have in common with Degas' early Ingres-like manner—elegance of hand, subtlety of light and shade, profound anatomical knowledge.

Degas urged his own application to drawing upon others. Camille Pissarro, writing to his son Lucien, who was then taking a course of drawing under Legros in England, said 'Degas says there is one way of escaping Legros' influence . . . to reproduce in your own place, from memory, the drawing you make in class. The drawing will have art—it will be your own—this is a good way of escaping slavish imitation.'

The antithesis of Degas in every way, Renoir painted as naturally as Degas drew. It was only by a strong effort of will and a stern attempt at self-discipline in the prime of life that Renoir first seriously applied himself to drawing. The immediate cause was self-discouragement—the feeling that he could go no farther along the path he had travelled—and this was reinforced by a visit to Italy in which he was particularly impressed by the works of Raphael. On his return to France he set himself to learn as much as he could from the study of Ingres and the French tradition. To this effort we owe the magnificent series of preliminary studies for his large composition 'The Bathers'. To achieve a monumental effect he based his composition on part of an eighteenth-century bas-relief of nymphs sculpted by Girardon round a fountain at Versailles. These tributes to the past and the grand manner were thought reactionary by Renoir's fellow Impressionists, but the century produced nothing of more intoxicating exuberance or sensual grace than these three nudes, moulded in attitudes of abandoned delight (Plates 10 and 11). Renoir's inborn vitality is intensified in these drawings through the control to which it has been subjected. These girls are bathers in the Seine, city workers from Paris of no higher *milieu* than Courbet's 'Baigneuses', and fit companions for the lads in Seurat's 'Baignade', but they have become universal and monumental by being caught in the ample rhythms of Renoir's great design.

In his later drawings, notably those carried out in sanguine, Renoir returned to the looser and more tolerant conception of form which was natural to him. The bodies of his models have escaped from the corset of the Ingres style and overflow in a riot of rounded and luscious curves. But the other drawing which represents him in this selection precedes that final phase of his style; it is a subject such as Degas drew, but invested with the haunting charm and surrender to femininity of which Renoir was not in the least afraid (Plate 23).

Fantin-Latour commemorated the early days of the Impressionist movement in his portrait group of 1870, 'The Studio of Batignolles'; but in spite of his friendship with Manet, Whistler, Renoir, Bazille and Monet he had little inclination to seek out for himself a position of isolation or independence. He was neither a painter of the open air nor a student of movement and moving light; indeed he had a horror of violent movement of any kind. He said to his English friend Edwin Edwards that he always wished 'to paint portraits of people side by side, to make the best possible study of heads and hands, and the folds of draperies'.

He loved to draw flowers because of their absolute stillness; and portraiture is absent from his later work because he found himself no longer capable of the strain it caused him. By that time he had become an enthusiast for music, and in many imaginative lithographs he made a not unsuccessful attempt to translate into graphic art the feelings aroused in him by symphonies and operas. In common with Baudelaire he had a great admiration for Wagner, whom the Impressionists regarded sympathetically as a fellow-revolutionary and outcast. In these lithographs by Fantin-Latour on musical themes there is a freedom and rhythm of line which recalls the dramatic upsurge of the Romantics; but the portrait study and still life reproduced in Plates 16 and 28 are of his early naturalistic and immobile manner. The young girl bending quietly over her sewing is said to be the artist's sister Nathalie; of her and his other sister Fantin-Latour made more than one double portrait. These portraits and this drawing date from the years when the artist was studying in Courbet's studio; in their sensitiveness to the play of light over a quiet and homely scene they are among the most attractive works to which the movement of Realism gave rise.

Pissarro was the co-ordinating element in the Impressionist movement, the only one of them to exhibit at each of the eight exhibitions held by the group, consistently single-minded in purpose and not deflected from his chosen path of independence by continued hardships. Even his temporary divagation into *pointillisme* was evidence of the open-minded attitude he adopted toward any new theory which he thought might have the seeds of truth in it; and when he found that the method was unsuited to him and had been a distorting influence on his style he had the courage to return to his natural 'Romantic-Impressionist' manner. But with all his openness of mind and staunch revolutionary outlook he was as insistent as Ingres that drawing was the basis of painting. Quotation has already been made from the letters he wrote to his son Lucien, who was studying art in England: these are full of such phrases as 'It is only by drawing often, drawing everything, drawing incessantly, that one fine day you discover to your surprise that you have rendered something in its true character.'

Camille Pissarro's own practice in drawing was as diverse as his painting. At times he draws pastoral scenes lightly tinted with watercolour in a way which anticipates the coloured woodcuts Lucien Pissarro made for the Eragny Press. Even when he draws peasant girls of a type and in a manner reminiscent of Millet, his treatment is lighter, less heavy and altogether sunnier in conception (Plate 5).

There could be no clearer instance of the effect of Japanese methods of composition on the art of the period than the portrait of Père Tanguy by Pissarro (Plate 12). The contour, over which the pressure of the chalk has been modified to suggest depth, and the shading, are in a purely occidental idiom; but the position of the kneeling form on the paper and its relation to the left-hand edge is copied verbatim from some Japanese print of an actor. The borrowings of Degas and Whistler from such motifs were scarcely ever on so literal a level.

Through his contacts with neo-Impressionism Pissarro forms as it were a link between the more orthodox Impressionists and Cézanne, the apostle of post-Impressionism. From the very first Cézanne's drawings had shown a careful and anxious regard for three-dimensional, sculptural form. The study of a male nude (Plate 13), from his academic period, shows how firmly this trait was already developed in him. The student who devoted this amount of energy to defining the volumes of the human form and fixing them plastically with violent contrasts of light and shade was not one to be content with the more superficial elements of construction in the landscape or its purely transient features of atmosphere and colour. Unlike Monet, who could paint the same hayrick at fifteen different moments of the day, he would seek, like the idealist philosophers, for the one universal hayrick behind these changing appearances. And so, day after day, he devoted himself to the mastery of his motif in which the Mont Sainte Victoire is suspended above the plains of Aix 'as a wave of the sea turned back by song'. To do Poussin over again after Nature he found it better to try to get to the bottom of one motif than to paint or draw a variety of novel scenes. A keen analyst in a practical way of his own vision—though his cryptic utterances have caused not a little subsequent confusion in aesthetic theory—he was worried by the paradox that the contour of a drawn object sets a rigid limit to its form whereas the object itself spreads beyond and behind that limit. 'Drawing is merely the outline of what you see,' he said, and again, 'Draw; but it is the reflection which *envelops*; light, through the general reflection, is the envelope.' To these perplexities are due the double and treble outlines which characterize his later drawings; he endeavours to show the roundness of the apple or of the plaster cast by caressing its edge with his pencil and, as it were, looking round it.

Colour is so integral a part of Cézanne's pictures, in which it virtually takes the place of perspective, that when he limits himself to pencil drawing he abstracts an essential element from his art. None the less these drawings show most instructively how his mind clutched out for the essential skeleton of construction in the motif. Both the landscape drawing of his Impressionist period (Plate 20) and the still life of his last phase (Plate 21) show him manipulating the pencil line as he does the dark tones in his painting to suggest the outlines of objects and the way they are painted. For all their box of bricks construction and solidity of effect, in them is imprisoned the same surging baroque fantasy that inspired his paintings of bathers and such compositions as 'The Rape'.

In an age of revolutionary painters Seurat was one of the most revolutionary, in an age of theorists the most ruthless theorist. The scheme of *pointillisme*, which lies at the basis of his neo-Impressionism and was founded on the researches into colour made by Chevreul when he was Director of the Gobelins tapestry works, does not directly concern us here. We may however note in passing how appropriate it is that optical laws with such an origin should produce paintings so closely resembling tapestries, and also that the merit of those paintings lies not in the theory to which they were cut but in Seurat's own sense of style, and the architectonic ability which enables him to make a monumental composition out of the proletarian scenes which interested him in the suburbs and on the river banks near Paris.

In contrast to the rarity of the paintings he completed in his tragically short life he left a surprisingly large bulk of drawings, and these are among the most original creations of the period. When these are preliminary studies for his paintings they show how carefully thought out was every detail. Improvisation was abhorrent to him. Rather than make a *pentimento* he would repeat a drawing with one feature only in a slightly different place. The clothes of the youth in the centre of 'La Baignade' were the subject of a study as meticulous as the drapery study of a follower of Leonardo da Vinci. The resemblance ends however in the degree of application, for the Old Master would have arranged his drapery to receive broad lighting and would define its edges and folds with sharp lines; Seurat studies the emergence of tone, with the emphasis on the complete dark. The academic nude (Plate 17) is an exception in his mature work for its comparative sharpness of definition, yet even here the effect is tenebrous. In a more characteristic drawing, such as the 'Group of people in front of a house' (Plate 37), an atmosphere of complete mystery is contrived. That we are in the suburbs which excited Seurat more than country or fashionable boulevards is shown by the factory chimney on the left; but the purpose of this huddle of figures, whether they are workmen having a lunch hour break or plotters planning theft or revolution by moonlight, remains ambiguous and adds to the tension of its effect. Had the pictures for which it is a study been executed it may well have been a bright hieratic composition in the manner of 'La Grande Jatte'.

Seurat shared a taste for popular entertainments with Degas, Lautrec, and Steinlen among the other typical representatives of his age. 'At the *Concert Européen*' (Plate 33) belongs to a series of drawings of cabarets and music halls which he carried out about 1887 on these themes, apparently in anticipation of a painting similar to 'La Parade' and 'Le Chahut'. In its highly abstract and balanced pattern, in the effective contrast between the lighted background and dark foreground, and in the touch of whimsicality which Seurat has given to the exaggerated coiffures of the time this is one of his most interpretive and effective compositions.

With considerable reason Dutch critics are beginning to contest the customary absorption of Van Gogh into the École de Paris. They point to the fact that almost six of his ten years of artistic activity belong to the 'Dutch period' into which a medley of influences and enthusiasms entered, among them that of the English illustrators of low life, besides Millet, Israels, Mauve and Mesdag. The ambition to paint works with a message in the style of these masters remained with Van Gogh to the end. Certainly the drawings and paintings of peasants and weavers which he made between the years 1880 and 1886 are unmistakably Dutch in origin and feeling; their technique is fully adequate to their almost oppressive truthfulness, but by themselves they could not have raised their author above the ranks of the secondary artists. It was personal contact in Paris with the leaders of the Impressionist and neo-Impressionist movements, with

Pissarro, Degas, Gauguin and Seurat, that shivered his dark earthy palette into fragments of the most vivid colour and transformed his drawing from a literal transcription of sordidness into a dancing, Bacchic shorthand. Good boys are the worst rebels in the end, and the most conventional schooling lies behind these calligraphic explosions. Bargue's 'Cours de Dessin', with its copies of Gérôme, Bougereau, and so forth, has already been cited as one of the first and perhaps the chief of Van Gogh's drawing masters; a large collection of prints and wood-engravings after Millet, Tenniel, Herkomer and Boughton was another. Nor did Van Gogh disdain, even in his Arles period, the help of mechanical aids such as the perspective frame, and he too made the effort to reproduce his visual experiences from memory.

The drawing of cottages at Les Saintes-Maries-de-la-Mer (Plate 18) was made in June 1888, when Van Gogh was spending a week by the Mediterranean, the most southerly point of his starved Northern search for the sun. Drawn in the heyday of his Arles period the swift straight brush strokes of which it is composed take in the scene with the exhaustive economy of a Chinese pen drawing. All that is represented is a poor assemblage of cottages such as might have been found in Drenthe or Neunen, but Van Gogh's drawings of those places did not speak as this does of his abandonment to the joy of living beneath that torrid and all-revealing sun. Less than a year later in the 'Stone seat in the hospital garden' (Plate 19) the mood has changed from exultation to a more profound and moving despair. The hospital is the asylum at St Rémy into which Van Gogh had voluntarily entered, and this drawing was made in the month of his arrival. Closed contours and curling strokes have replaced the arrow straight lines of his happier days. Some have sought to see in these troubled waving curves, which enter into his later painting like disturbed magnetic fields of force, a reflection of his disordered mind, which was always at this time on the verge of madness. But that is to misconceive the nature of his insight. When he spoke of himself as possessed by a 'terrible lucidity' he was, consciously or not, laying bare the elements of his creation. Fundamentally a vessel of the religious spirit, he was seeking for an art which would cradle the unquiet spirit of man to sleep, which could console and at the same time ennoble him. He could not do that by taking thought; but by straining his body and mind to seize his intuitions before they faded, he did note down visions of which the universality is now fully recognized. Such insight is often more active in sickness than in health, and may be withheld from the sane but granted to the insane. It is to be found here in the haunting melancholy of the scene, of which Van Gogh's verbal description is also eloquent—'a new canvas . . . as ordinary as a chromo in the little shops, which represents the eternal nests of greenery for lovers. Some thick trunks covered with ivy, the ground also covered with ivy and periwinkle, a stone bench and a bush of roses pale in the cold shadow. In the foreground some plants with a white calix. It is a green violet and rose. . . Since I have been here the deserted garden, planted with large pines beneath which grows the grass, tall and unkempt and mixed with various weeds, has sufficed for my work'.

The personality and career of Gauguin are as fascinating as Van Gogh's, though for very different reasons. It must always remain an enigma how this matter-of-fact, over-bearing, stiff-necked man, who turned to painting from business comparatively late in life, should have found within himself the key to a modern magic and wild romance. His flight to Tahiti was a Byronic gesture more in keeping with the world of Delacroix and Decamps than his more matter-of-fact times. 'One paints so well at Batignolles' Renoir said when invited to accompany him to the South Sea islands. But Gauguin did not paint so well at Batignolles or Pont-Aven as he did in the exotic distances. Surprisingly few painters have found profit for their art in the earthly paradise of the South Sea islands. William Hodges, who accompanied Cook on his second voyage to Tahiti, was able, with-in the limitations possible to a style based upon Richard Wilson, to express the glories of these islands in the unspoiled day of their first discovery; and Gauguin is almost the only painter to surpass him.

Gauguin was free of the horror of a literary element in painting which was induced in the Impressionists by the excesses of the academic school. He set out to achieve deliber-ately what Van Gogh had done by instinct, to make of his paintings poems and haunting melodies which spoke directly to the primitive and unconscious in man. He knew that to subserve this end any device was legitimate, the heightening of colour, its symbolic and decorative use, the deliberate distortion of form and contour. In Martinique and Tahiti he found a sufficient residue of primitive simplicity to fertilize his imagination with the subjects of his large metaphysical murals; the luxuriant colouring of the vegetation and the remote mask-like features of the native races provided the symbols he needed for self-expression.

Gauguin is not regarded primarily as a draughtsman, but design is in a very real sense the basis of his work. Through his woodcuts his sense of form had a great effect on Munch and the German Expressionists. He sought for flatness in his paintings, but their cunningly deformed contours and decoratively contrived rhythms are a highly mannered and personal drawing. He urged close study of the silhouette of every object—'distinct-ness of outline is that attribute of the hand that is not engulfed by any hesitation of the will'—and favoured working from memory as a means of generalizing and avoiding a baleful excess of detail. He attached great importance to his sketches and studies; they were so intimate a revelation that he was secretive about them. 'A critic at my house sees some paintings,' he wrote in *Avant et Après*. 'Greatly perturbed, he asks for my drawings. My drawings? Never! They are my letters, my secrets.' Such a sheet as that bearing studies of Tahitians (Plate 39) might for its enigmatical content bear the title he gave to the pictures which summed up his experience 'Whence do we come? What are we? Whither are we going?'

The drawings of Toulouse-Lautrec lead straight to the heart of the 'nineties, that fabulous *fin-de-siècle* when the ways of France and England for a moment converged in decadence. Degas influenced the subjects on which he concentrated, the music hall and every other kind of entertainment in the abundant night life of Paris, but the biting satanism of treatment was Toulouse-Lautrec's alone. His whole life was a series of manias, a mania for observing life in brothels and among Lesbians, a mania for bars and music halls, and for the drink which finally led him to ruin. Above all he had a mania for drawing what he saw in the haunts to which his incessant curiosity for such subjects led him, especially the dancers of Montmartre, Jane Avril, La Goulue, May Milton. Even his painting is a sort of drawing, with the same linear touch and angular brush strokes. Like Degas he seized upon the dramatic and unfamiliar aspect of a face when the source of light comes from below—as from the footlights—and elevated this into a permanent mannerism of his style. He built palpably upon the lessons of the Japanese print which had been current in France for over thirty years.

The drawing reproduced in Plate 14 is one of Toulouse-Lautrec's many representations of La Goulue, a celebrated dancer of the Moulin Rouge and other cabarets. Toulouse-Lautrec, who was always good at drawing people's backs, apparently found hers a particularly expressive one. Her partner is Valentin le Désossé, or Boneless, who owed his name to his extreme suppleness. This extraordinary creature, whose grimacing features are among the most comic ever delineated, is said to have been of good family and to have had intellectual acquaintances. He is thus a typical member of the cosmopolitan underworld among which Toulouse-Lautrec moved, and among which he himself must be numbered—a descendant of the Counts of Toulouse drinking himself to death in the squalid haunts of Montmartre. For all its masterly economy the drawing does not conceal the abandoned vulgarity which lies below the surface comedy; but the beat of the dance and the absorption of the actor-dancers are perfectly conveyed. No one knew better than Toulouse-Lautrec that his subjects were laid in a world where unglamorous vice and violent realities lay just below an apparent gaiety of heart; and of that world he has produced an image of hallucinatory vividness.

The draughtsmen so far represented have, with the exception of Daumier, been men whose *métier* was that of painter. The work of Toulouse-Lautrec leads us to a group in the 'nineties, of whom Forain and Steinlen are the chief, in which the balance is reversed. One predisposing factor for the success of this group was the wave of journalistic expansion which took place at about this time, particularly in illustrated periodicals. Their forerunners comprise such figures as Grandville and Doré; but hitherto the most outstanding French artist to practise solely as an illustrator was Constantin Guys. Born in the first decade of the nineteenth century, he is the indispensable chronicler of the Second Empire, the gay, prosperous, artificial world of parade and levity which came into being when he was forty-five. The course of his formative years is scarcely known; he fought at Missolonghi, and his wanderings led him to the Near East. It appears that his first professional engagement was with the *Illustrated London News*, when he was in England; in this way he became a colleague of Leech's, and their mutual influence was such that their drawings have been confused. He went to Spain in the 'forties and again in the 'fifties. The *Illustrated London News* enabled him to revisit the Near East and scenes of soldiering by sending him as a war correspondent to the Crimea in 1854; but he returned to Paris in good time to gorge his vision on the spectacle of the Second Empire before its collapse in 1870.

It was a time when dissipation and frivolity were deliberately promoted by the Emperor to distract people's minds from their loss of political liberty. Paris became an outdoor stage in the daytime and an indoor stage at night. Aided by an admirable visual memory Guys assisted constantly at this spectacle, noting down avidly the promenade in the Bois de Boulogne, meetings in the Champs Elysées, the carriages in the streets, fashionable women in their boxes at the theatre, the levées at the Imperial Court. Baudelaire said of him that he had the incessant curiosity and joy in life of a permanently convalescent man. But out of all these scenes in which he delighted he had above all a passion for drawing horses and a passion for drawing women.

The sketch of a spirited pair of horses drawn up by a proud coachman outside a country house (Plate 36) might have been made as an illustration to the second act of *La Traviata*, so absolute is the conviction with which it places us back into the 'fifties. Indeed there is, as a rarity among his work, an actual operatic illustration, a drawing of the graveyard scene in *Don Giovanni* as he had seen it in a contemporary performance (Plate 41).

Of women he portrayed every kind from elegant ladies of fashion (Plate 32) to the rough companions of the *apache*. But above all he was fascinated more and more by the denizens of the *maisons publiques* and *maisons closes*. Swathed in voluminous folds of skirts, displaying the curiously shapeless symbols which did duty for legs in the days when it was improper to see them, reclining on sofas and receiving the respectful homage of their admirers, these decorations of red plush and gilt, gas-lighted Venus-bergs fill us with nostalgia for an utterly irrecoverable past. Some critics not displeased by the naughtiness of condoning sin have written as though Guys were a satanist wallowing in filth of the most shocking degradation. In their own day his drawings of brothels must have seemed matter-of-fact to those who were familiar with such interiors and 'broad' to those who were not; but now they have a simple charm of *mise-en-scène* which completely disarms any ethical inquiry. It is the sardonic and ruthless eye of Toulouse-Lautrec which has preserved for ever the rottenness of perversion and vice; and there may well have been greater opportunities for such a record as his in the 'nineties than at any time before or since.

For, although the 'nineties were in a sense the gay 'nineties they were also the solemn 'nineties. Increasingly, in Germany and Great Britain as well as in France, the pre-occupation of writers and artists with the inequalities of human resources became apparent. They were obsessed by the ironic and poignant contrast between the very rich and the very poor. Therefore rich and poor alike would go to cabarets to hear Aristide Bruant sing his sentimental songs about the tragedies of proletarian love, and applauded *apache* sketches and dancers in the music halls. This awakening of social conscience was often crude, often wearisome and usually propagandist. In so far as it becomes a genuine artistic manifestation it is represented in England by the work of Phil May and, somewhat later, in Germany by the Simplizissimus artists. Forain and

Steinlen are the most important exponents of the movement in France.

Forain's savage indictment of society is more irresponsible than Steinlen's. The anti-Dreyfusard campaign he conducted recalls the worst excesses of *Der Stürmer*, and a persistent anti-Semitism remains a most regrettable feature of his character. His treatment of the seamy side of life however is fully as disillusioned and unpitying as that of Toulouse-Lautrec. The many drawings of prostitution he made for *La Comédie Parisienne* underline remorselessly the commercial aspect of the situation. His little girls have none of the romantic appeal of those drawn by Gavarni or Guys. It was to such a pass that the cult of realism had led; to start with the assumption that everything is appropriate material for art, and that art is created simply by the translation of life, is to be driven to dwell upon the unpleasant to the exclusion of the pleasant, and the ugly at the expense of the beautiful. However, no one can question the pointedness and masterly directness of Forain's reporting (Plates 15 and 25), and in his legal scenes he enters legitimately into Daumier's succession.

Steinlen is consistently a socialist in his outlook. Known as the artist of Montmartre from his exclusive residence in that district he displays a profound sympathy with the oppressed, tinged with bitterness toward their oppressors. He was a poster designer of almost comparable distinction with Toulouse-Lautrec; and in 'Dans la Rue' he has set more than 100 illustrations to the ditties in Parisian argot which Bruant used to sing at his cabaret. The songs, with their mixture of self-conscious toughness and sentiment, their recurrent shrug of the shoulders, have lost their appeal; but the illustrations, and most of Steinlen's other studies of the life of the poor, have retained their actuality. The striking composition of 'Two masons watching a funeral' (Plate 34) is one of two known studies for a lithograph in *Gil Blas* illustrating a song by Maurice Boukay called 'Tu t'en iras, le pieds devant'. A verse of the song is worth quoting here, not for its intrinsic merit, but because it gives so well the flavour of those self-deprecating serio-comic compositions which scarcely even the genius of Yvette Guilbert could now make acceptable:

> *Tu t'en iras, les pieds devant*
> *Ainsi que tous ceux de ta race*
> *Grand homme qu'un souffle terrasse*
> *Comme le pauvre fou qui passe*
> *Et, sous la lune, va rêvant*
> *De beauté, de gloire éternelles*
> *Du ciel cherché dans les prunelles*
> *Au rythme pur des villanelles.*

Inadequate though its expression may be, this is in the same mood as Laforgue and the early work of T. S. Eliot. Steinlen's conception of the two masons perched on their dizzy height above the funeral embodies his own far robuster outlook; it is a scene of Doré's brought closer to reality.

Steinlen's customarily stern and sombre view of life is, surprisingly, diversified by his love of cats. His houses in Montmartre were always full of his pets, and he delighted to draw them as decorations for posters or in comic strips. Not that they are always as sleek and intelligent as the one portrayed in Plate 35; in the comic strips, sad to relate, many are betrayed by their curiosity or their tempers into violent and horrible ends. But in this he was following a formula common to Caran d'Ache, Willette, and the other strip cartoonists of the decade.

The mystic dreamy universe of Odilon Redon is a reminder—if reminder is needed in the age of *Les Fleurs du Mal*—that all was not healthy and matter-of-fact in the drawing rooms of the Boulevard Hausmann. He is of a different kinship from the other independent painters; of the lineage of Bosch and Breughel and a precursor of the Surrealists. Fantin-Latour taught him lithography, in which he expressed most fluently those strange illogical combinations, of faces with enormous eyes floating on the sea, of flowers and trees, which bring into the world of forms something of the emotions he found in music. Even when he draws a profile only, or a bunch of flowers, it has some indefinable quality of madness or other-worldliness, illumined as it may be by the light of a spiritualistic materialization, or distorted with the workings of his subconscious mind. His drawing is an exploration, as by means of a planchette, of the unknown and unsuspected possibilities beyond the normal powers of the senses; and under Redon's direction the message it gave was *un frisson nouveau*, a valid and original emotion. Yet, so conservative were the times in their outlook on drawing that even Redon regretted that he had not explored the academic approach to the full: 'Were I allowed to start over again today my education as a painter, I think that for the growth and the greater development of my faculties I should do many copies of the human body. I should dissect it, analyse it and even model it.'—So he expresses the very programme Degas carried out for himself.

The cornucopia of French art which pours from this rich half-century almost smothers the contribution to drawing of many other talented artists—Carrière, Carpeaux, Tissot and the Belgian draughtsman Rops. A further word may be spared for Charles Bargue, whose contribution to Van Gogh's development has already been noted, if only for the sake of drawing attention to his delightful 'Artist and his model' (Plate 24). This composition study for a painting in the style of Meissonier is of a quite unexpected charm, as though the spirit of the eighteenth century which it represents had for a moment taken possession of the hand that drew it.

Both the Impressionists and post-Impressionists paid a somewhat grudging tribute of admiration to Puvis de Chavannes. Even if they did not like the allegorical subjects— Summer, Winter, Peace, War, Ave Picardia Nutrix and the like—with which he decorated the walls of so many public buildings in Paris, the provinces, and even the Boston Library, and admired still less the archaic style in which he treated these themes, they had to admit the extreme sureness of his drawing and his skilful decorative sense (Plate 30). Gauguin, for instance, had Puvis de Chavannes in his mind when engaged on

31

his own large mural composition, even if he was conscious only of repudiating his methods and outlook.

The election of a Frenchman as Professor of Fine Art at University College might have had an enlivening effect on the whole course of English art; but the influence of Legros, who was appointed to this post in 1876, was responsible for its further decline into an unambitious provincialism. His pencil portraits of contemporaries, though they showed his painstaking study of Holbein, are of a repellent grey weakness and often not even good likenesses. The 'Nude Study' represents his timid academicism at its most favourable (Plate 31 bottom).

The most potent energy at work in Europe at the close of the century was, however, that of the sixty-year-old Rodin. He threw himself into drawing with all the vivacity of a sculptor liberated from the hard unyielding pressure of his customary material. A pupil of Lecoq de Boisbaudran, he made the most successful use of his teacher's method for freeing the model from the constraint of classroom attitudes. Unclothed they wandered freely around the Hotel Byron and in its grounds; they sat down, lay down, indulged in acrobatics. Out of this full gamut of the range of attitudes possible to the human frame Rodin would choose any improvisation which appealed to him and fix it in his instantaneous notation. The vagaries of this swift, corrected line, which does not always return directly upon itself, show that he kept his eyes on his model the whole time. Then he would give the drawings the semblance of flesh with a warm reddish brown wash: indifferent to the original pose he would discuss with his friends whether the drawings looked better upside down or sideways; that having been decided, he gave many of them fanciful titles. Like his more 'curious' sculptures these drawings are an embodiment of his inexhaustible sensuous appreciation of life and, predominantly, of the human body. He saw no reason to conceal the fact that he was always in a state of high physical excitement, and his innumerable sketches embody his intense epicurean appreciation, and are at the same time a revelation of the fathomless variety of human loveliness. It is not loveliness of a conventional kind; Rodin does not idealize; he gives summary, coarse features to his girls, and twists and contorts them in the wildest attitudes. Yet, for all their apparent insouciance the two nudes (Plates 27 and 29) are complete three-dimension statements of form, as strenuous and reposeful as the 'Dancing Sivas' Rodin admired. Into 'The Embrace' (Plate 26) he has poured the whole of passionate abandonment—the strength and weakness described by Swinburne in the words he puts into the mouth of Sappho:

> *The intolerable infinite desire*
> *Made my face pale like faded fire*
> *When the ashen pyre falls through with heat.*

The English School

★

ENGLISH drawings in the second half of the nineteenth century come from three main groups: the Pre-Raphaelites and their followers, the neo-Classicists, and the professional illustrators. The first noteworthy fact about this classification is the negative one that it contains no landscape draughtsmen as such. The school of English watercolourists had flourished for a century; and though there had never been so many practising the craft as in the years following 1850, and their work was avidly collected, it is only too apparent that the virtue had gone out of this once vigorous art. The failure was partly one of technique; a mistaken idea of progress had led to the use of more and brighter colours, and the aim became to make watercolours as like oil painting as possible—an ambition in which the artists were greatly assisted by the large scale on which they worked and the heavy gilt mounts and mouldings which framed their pictures. So the tinted vapour and coloured steam in which Turner composed his empyrean fantasies degenerated into Birket Foster's niggling stipples of rustic prettinesses, and the broad washes of Cotman languished into Frederick Walker's ochreous confections. The Pre-Raphaelites mishandled watercolour as balefully as anyone else; but at least they sought to express by its means the same other-worldly vision as can be found in their oil paintings and, more purely still, in their black-and-white drawings.

The visitor to the private rooms in Burlington House will see on one wall a painting by Hogarth of the Life Drawing Class of the St Martin's Academy, and facing it a painting by Zoffany of the Cast Room of the Royal Academy. The students in the former are grouped around a well-developed male model, whose Carracciesque posture displays somewhat artificially the muscular rhythms of his body; in the latter they endeavour by the aid of exiguous candle-light to copy the most familiar classical casts. These two paintings summarize the customary method of instruction, as it had been formalized in the academies and artists' studios of Italy in the sixteenth century. With this background and from these models Etty laboured and Mulready produced the highly finished life studies which are among the best English drawings of the first half-century. It was in the Royal Academy cast room however that Holman Hunt met Millais and started that series of conversations which led to a new departure in English art. For, just as landscape drawing had lost its savour so had English academic instruction become weak and characterless. The students were left very much to their own devices, to profit under their own initiative if they could, but otherwise to idle away their time and pupate half formed and badly taught.

In fact, the years round 1850 mark a complete break in our native school, not merely through the conscious initiative taken as a group by the Pre-Raphaelites but also in the other developments of drawing. The neo-Classics were then seeking their decisive training abroad; Stevens and Watts in Italy, Leighton in Italy, France and Germany, and Poynter in Italy and France, obtaining in this way a first-hand acquaintanceship with the sculptures and paintings which would influence their maturer work. The manner of the illustrators also underwent a remarkable change. The virile and robust social criticism of Cruikshank and Phiz, founded upon eighteenth-century English caricature, and expressed in the same vigorous calligraphy, was repudiated by authors and public alike. The accurate delineation of respectability replaced the Rabelaisean interpretation of low life and eccentric character. Leech made *Punch* fit for every drawing-room by limiting his range of jokes to foreigners, seasickness and the precocity of the young; Tenniel imitated the austere outline of the German Nazarenes, Du Maurier was trained in Gleyre's studio, and the Pre-Raphaelites themselves made outstanding illustrations which led to the radically different appearance of the books of the 'sixties.

The predisposing reasons for this shift of interest and style were complex and various. For one thing the Romantic movement, which had dominated English intellectual life for sixty or seventy years, had spent its first impetus and was declining into a new, more self-conscious and less spontaneous phase. Historical study, which had hitherto been the humble handmaid of Romanticism, became its mistress. A larger and more varied past was recreated to provide a fresh sphere of historical subjects. It was of more importance to dress the characters of former days in clothing resembling their true costume and to surround them with the right sort of furniture and architecture. The Tractarian movement and the Gothic revival pointed the way to a renewal of interest in medievalism, and the ugliness of the modern industrial civilization was a further incentive for fantasy to place its constructions in that dimly realized golden age. The Pre-Raphaelites therefore sought to father their very modern malaise of spirit upon the historical or literary characters of the Middle Ages.

The Classicists and neo-Classicists were of like temper, but they too felt the need to escape from present realities into a golden past. In placing their golden age in the 'glory that was Greece and the grandeur that was Rome' they were following a longer established practice than the Pre-Raphaelites; but they too were responsive to the requirements of historic accuracy which their age made of them, and to the latest historical research bearing on that demand. The predominant place given to classical studies in English education entailed that their public was not ignorant of the stories of which they treated, and was alert to solecisms but appreciative of success. Though the Elgin Marbles and Greek vase painting were heavily drawn on for incidentals and accessories, these models did transfuse a certain classical elegance and grace into their most able copyists.

Keats is often cited to countenance the Pre-Raphaelites in their choice of medieval subject matter; but his treatment of classical themes in a Romantic fashion can as fairly be instanced to justify the neo-Classic movement.

Illustrators were obliged to be versatile, since they might be required to make a drawing for a Viking saga or German ballad one week and for a story or song of contemporary life the next. Unlike the Pre-Raphaelite paintings, which were generally more effective in treating of medieval themes, these factual illustrations are our most precious source for the social history of Victorian life; but by the time 'period' illustration had become a virtual science in the hands of Hugh Thomson the great days of popular illustration were over.

For all its travelling in time and space the English school retained its markedly national character. The subtle insular temper which had been reflected in the change of style in Van Dyck in the seventeenth century was still able to prevail upon the style of Tissot in the nineteenth century. What that temper was is partly revealed by Baudelaire in his article on the Salon of 1859. Regretting the absence of an English section he says: 'Ainsi, ardeurs tragiques, gesticulations à le Kean et à la Macready, intimes gentillesses du *home*, splendeurs orientales réfléchies dans le poétique miroir de l'esprit anglais, verdures écossaises, fraîcheurs enchanteresses, profondeurs fuyantes des aquarelles grandes comme de décors, quoique si petites, nous ne vous contemplerons pas.' The self-conscious gulf between English and Continental art is further illustrated by the remarks made by Richard Redgrave in 1893: 'Art in England has flourished from the demands of those who love it as a home delight; therefore our pictures are small, and suited to our private residences, while the subjects are such as we can live by and love; and hence, they have been largely illustrative of the feelings and affections of our land, and of the beautiful nature of which we desire to be reminded as a solace in the moments of rest from the hard labour of daily life. . . . The contrast between the British and Continental artists in their choice of subject was singularly apparent in the vast gathering in Paris in 1855. To pass from the grand salons appropriated in the Palais des Beaux Arts to French and Continental works, into the long gallery of British pictures, was to pass at once from the midst of warfare and its incidents, from passion, strife and bloodshed, from martyrdoms and sufferings, to the peaceful scenes of home—it was said of our pictures that they reflected the life of a people who had long been permitted to dwell safely.' This summing-up refers more particularly to the painting of the earlier part of the century, but that there was a constant distinguishing factor is confirmed by Delacroix's comments on the Pre-Raphaelite movement:

'I have been struck by that prodigious conscience that this people can introduce even into works of imagination; it even seems that in returning to excess of detail they are more in their element than when they imitate, above all, the Italian painters and the Flemish colourists. . . . They are always English under this apparent transformation. Instead of making pastiches, pure and simple, of the Italian primitives, as has become the fashion with us, they mingle with the manner of the old schools a sentiment infinitely personal.' That *sentiment infiniment personnel* is to be found equally in the *Arabian Nights* of Boyd Houghton, the *Salome* of Beardsley, and the Grecian compositions of Leighton, Poynter and Moore.

Although he was not the originator, Rossetti was the dominant member of the Pre-Raphaelites while the group held together. Soon after he took up art he was conscious of a weakness in drawing; but the methods adopted by Madox Brown to cure him of this fault, by setting him in front of still life and telling him to paint it, only bored and exasperated him. Holman Hunt proved a wiser teacher by setting him at work on a large painting and telling him to treat the details as he came to them. For, although he was technically deficient, Rossetti had a vivid visual imagination, and its workings are embodied more directly in his sketches than in his finished watercolours or oil paintings. Like the character in one of the poems of Poe that captivated him, he 'watched the pale sheeted ghosts go by'. His visionary pageant was peopled from the poems and legends of past times: *Faust, Hamlet* and, above all, *The Divine Comedy*. At first he sought to express his visions in the manner of Maclise, voluptuous drawings in which originality of content is masked by the patently derivative style. Then, with the illustrations to Poe's 'Raven' and 'Dante drawing his first Angel' he first found himself. It is a Gothic idiom, in which angularity of line and a certain under-furnished archaism confess the Pre-Raphaelite creed. The discovery of Miss Siddal was a final stage in his approach to mastery. She was for him what a medium is for the inquirer into psychical research—the mediator of the spiritual world. She was the living embodiment of romantic love as he imagined it, and at the same time her sensual dreamy features seemed to him equally the perfect model for Beatrice or the Virgin Mary. As Christina wrote with devastating sisterly candour:

> *One face looks out from all his canvases,*
> *One selfsame figure sits or walks or leans . . .*
> *He feeds upon her face by day and night.*

But there is no monotony about the countless drawings Rossetti made of Miss Siddal. Apart from acting as a focus for his visions, she was an object of such interest to him that all his dilatoriness in working from other models or on his paintings disappeared in the absorption of drawing her standing at the window (Plate 43), sitting, reading, embroidering, kneeling, or playing the pipes—in a hundred poses and with the light falling on her form in every possible manner. Such is his concentration on the task of drawing her that his naturally diffuse style crystallizes and takes on a new power. Madox Brown wrote in his diary in 1855: 'He showed me a drawer full of "Guggums": God knows how many, but not bad work I should say for the six years he has known her: it is like a monomania with him. Many of them are matchless in beauty and one day will be worth large sums.'

The magnificent study drawn from Fanny Cornforth in about 1855 for the head of the woman in 'Found' (Plate 47 top) was the finest part of Rossetti's one unachieved painting on a modern theme. It transcribes the thing seen with complete fidelity, but in doing so loses none of the emotion conveyed to the mid-Victorian mind by the idea of a street-walker, outcast and destitute, being found by the lover of her childhood days.

When Miss Siddal died Rossetti lost his way. It is painful to behold the large crayon portrait drawings, in his later manner, of vacuous and bovine features of which the lips are swelled into a factitious semblance of sexual enticement. The handling is woolly and the sentiment vulgar; but it is by these works that Rossetti is all too often represented and judged in public collections.

Millais was always more at home than Rossetti in dealing with subjects taken from contemporary life. He is invariably stated to have departed in his later works from the Pre-Raphaelite manner; but in truth it is very hard to see how the difference in approach between for instance 'The North West Passage' (1874) and the 'Order of Release' (1853) is to be defined. The degree of naturalism is of the same order in either, and 'truth to nature' is one of the few formulable tenets of Pre-Raphaelitism. Sincerity of intention, which is the other main formula, was never a prime concern with Millais. He was a precocious youngster, endowed with immense technical gifts, but with a weak imagination. Again, if popular approval is to be taken as a criterion of what is or is not Pre-Raphaelite then the plain fact is that the group were left out in the wilderness for at most five years—they had an easy passage to fame compared with that of the Impressionists. It is true of course that as he grew more famous Millais painted more pot-boilers and often worked carelessly, and so did Rossetti; but when he exerted himself his guiding principles were the same in 1870 as in 1850.

That there was no sudden break in Millais' manner is clearly seen in the series of drawings for book-illustration which he executed in the 'fifties and 'sixties. In these commissions, where subject manner and mood were given to him he was adept at finding the image to join to them. He showed no awkwardness at combining the minutiae of modern furnishing and costume with the scenes of strong emotion which frequently enter into the novels of the mid-Victorian period and which were naturally chosen as the climaxes to be illustrated. Trollope's praise of his drawings for 'The Small House at Allington' was not misdirected. An instructive contrast between the ways of working dictated by Victorian ideas of propriety and those, for instance, of Rodin is provided by the story of the genesis of the 'Black Brunswicker', which represents a girl parting from her lover before the battle of Waterloo. Both figures were drawn by Millais from models, but they did not pose together: when Mrs Perugini was acting as model for the girl she embraced a lay figure; and the private of the Life Guards who posed for the Brunswicker had an equally unresponsive support.

There was however a time in Millais' early career, roughly coinciding with the Cyclographic Club and the period of close cohesion of the Pre-Raphaelite group, when he sought out subjects of the imagination, generally as designs for pictures. 'The Deluge' is a particularly vivid and impressive example of this class, in its dramatic composition and skilful rendering of approaching horror (Plate 44). His fine study from Miss Siddal for 'Ophelia' (Plate 46 top) is, despite its technical certitude, less moving than Rossetti's study for 'Found', with all its marks of painful conception; but the drawing 'Girls in a meadow' (Plate 45) has, for all its mannered quaintness, a quite exceptional charm.

Both Holman Hunt and Ford Madox Brown made distinguished isolated contributions to the illustration of the time, the former in Moxon's *Tennyson*, which gives a remarkable cross-section of the best book illustrations of the period. A painter and designer closely related to the Pre-Raphaelites who became more exclusively known as an illustrator was Arthur Hughes. When contrasted with his genuine appreciation of children and the delights of mother-love the coloured charades of Kate Greenaway are seen to be of very poor quality. In his paintings of 'The Tryst', 'The Long Engagement' and 'Home from the Sea' he showed himself able to represent ordinary people in strong emotional situations without recourse to exaggerated sentimentalism. The homeliness of the garden in which his heroine is smelling a flower, of the tree on which have been carved the initials now almost effaced by moss, or of the churchyard in which the sailor boy's mother has been buried, adds to the poignancy of the resignation, patience and grief which is his theme. The illustration to *Enoch Arden* (Plate 48) is a consummate example of this ability. The boy is Philip Ray, the undeclared lover of Annie Lee, who having seen her plight her troth to Enoch Arden

Groan'd
And slipt aside, and like a wounded life
Crept down into the hollows of the wood;
There, while the rest were loud in merrymaking
Had his dark hour unseen, and rose and past
Bearing a lifelong hunger in his heart.

The undergrowth of the wood is observed with true Pre-Raphaelite minuteness, but the attention to detail rather enhances than obscures the grief-stricken abandonment of the young man, in the way the eye can take an interest in the most trivial things when the heart is breaking. This close focus and nearness of vision, the integration of the figure and its surroundings into a concordant whole, is a quality in which Arthur Hughes excels.

Another artist who was greatly influenced by the Pre-Raphaelites and whose best work was done in the form of portrait drawings or designs for book illustration was Frederick Sandys. He was far from being exclusively the product of indigenous influences. His illustrations show not only that he knew the work of Dürer, but that he had learned from it how to adjust his drawing to the process of wood-engraving. Although he only designed some two dozen wood-engravings, each has become a classic embodiment of the 'sixties through his profound technical insight. He found also a more modern mentor in the wood-engravings of Alfred Rethel. This German artist of the schools of Düsseldorf and Frankfurt had produced, while he hovered between sanity and mental derangement, a series of drawings on the Dance of Death, suggested by the

Belgian resurrection of 1848. In these works of quite unusual expressive power the spirit as well as the theme of the German late medieval Dances of Death lives again. Sandys has put this manner to his own uses in such an illustration as 'Amor Mundi' where the troubadour and his mistress are singing and laughing, oblivious of the snakes at their feet and the woman's putrefying corpse in the foreground; and again in 'Yet once more on the organ play' in which the figure of Death stands behind the organ on which the musician is to play to the dying man. Sandys had a well-developed taste for the macabre and also for the salacious, and though their loss is most regrettable it is hardly surprising that drawings he prepared for the *Biblical Life of Joseph* were destroyed by a 'too prudish publisher'.

Of his published illustrations, 'If' is deservedly the most famous of all. In this illustration to Christina Rossetti's poem of female ennui:

> *If he would come to-day, to-day*
> *Oh what a day to-day would be*

the pose of the figure is adapted from Dürer's 'Melancholia'. Sandys left nothing to chance or happy improvisation in such illustrations: he made separate drawings from nature for the elements as well as the finished whole. The motif of a girl biting her hair had moreover a personal significance for him: it recurs in the pencil portrait called 'Proud Maisie' in the Victoria and Albert Museum.

Burne-Jones belongs to the second generation of the Pre-Raphaelites. It often happens in movements which rely on a specialized kind of imaginative sensibility that the original integrity loses much of its force in later manifestations; the mysticism become somnambulism, the poetry effeminacy. So it is with the work of Burne-Jones, despite its great success in his lifetime not only in England but Germany. Paintings which seemed in their day to be of an almost intolerable beauty now recall the folk-dancing of the aesthetic inhabitants of Bedford Park; his pallid, androgynous creatures display an exasperating lack of potency. This hesitation and failure to get to real grips with either the actual or the dream world are accentuated in Burne-Jones' drawings. A lack of technical capacity made him rejoice that in his idiom figures of any size could be placed without regard to the laws of perspective. The drawings, or rather scribbles, he made to illustrate the Kelmscott Press Chaucer had to be redrawn by Catterson-Smith or Fairfax Murray to fit them for reproduction. In his note-books and pencil portraits he adopts a light grey tint and a timidity of approach to form which convicts him of exhausted imagination and a fundamental lack of vitality. It is astonishing to recall that he retired from the Old Water Colour Society 'owing to a misunderstanding over his "Phyllis and Demophoon" to which some of the members took exception as being too undraped', for his drawings of women lead one to suppose that he had never seen the female form unclothed or at least was blind to its salient characteristics.

Watts is another draughtsman who is fundamentally unsatisfactory through his failure to face the realities of the human body. If a representational painter's message is dependent upon his representing Faith or Hope or Love and Death through an allegory composed of human bodies, he cannot without insincerity and failure censor those bodies, as Watts did, in the interests of his own lack of courage or public prudery.

No draughtsman could be farther from the reach of such reproaches than Alfred Stevens; indeed the fidelity with which he made nude studies of a favourite model was inevitably regarded in his day as shocking and earned him the reputation of immorality. Stevens alone is sufficient to prove that the whole of English art in the second half of the nineteenth century is not comprised in the work of the Pre-Raphaelites and their followers. If anything could be more impressive than his actual achievement, it is his complete isolation from his contemporary artists and from the collectors; he is a lonely and enigmatic figure in that age of self-assertion and bustle. His strange fits of indolence and his incorrigible procrastination in completing commissions were perhaps causes; and one of his biographers records that he could hardly find it in him to be polite to a Government official, which was an obvious disqualification for one who was supremely fitted for public commissions. Here surely was an artist who was ideally equipped to carry out official portraiture and sculpture of the highest level; but only the Wellington Monument in St Paul's stands as a magnificent torso of what he might have fulfilled.

His palpable admiration for Michelangelo does not make him a derivative Mannerist or pasticheur; rather he is a Renaissance artist born out of time, as Beddoes was an Elizabethan poet born into the nineteenth century. The spirit of the age facilitated the assimilation of Renaissance styles. A bust by J. Cockle Lucas was placed by Bode in the Kaiser Frederick Museum, Berlin, as an authentic work by Leonardo da Vinci, and Bastianini's remarkable forgeries of Renaissance sculpture are of the same epoch. Stevens himself was so adept a copyist of Italian bronzes that he deceived the foremost living experts. But this remarkable power of assimilating the formal language of another time was not limited to the Cinquecento. The drawings he made during his *Wanderjahre* after frescoes by Ghirlandaio, Gozzoli and Fra Angelico, some of which may be seen in the British Museum, are equally astonishing in their freedom from period flavour and their timeless comprehension of an earlier style. Though by preference he worked in the grand manner he left two or three most affecting portraits: Mrs Collman, Mrs Mitchell and her baby, and the drawing of a dead boy in the Tate Gallery.

Since he completed so little, his working drawings are all the more important. Whether they are designs for decoration, sculpture or painting they demonstrate his never-flagging inventiveness, his sure instinct for form, and his superb architectural sense. The plasticity of his figures is fully realized; energetic action is strongly expressed. His judgment on the relation of human figures to architecture and on the balance of ornament to the elements of design was unfailing; and he had the sort of grace which only goes with strength of conception and execution. His drawings alone are enough to mark him out as the most versatile, indeed the only all-round, artist of his century (Plates 56, 57 and 60). His influence on industrial design has been given less credit than that emanating from William Morris and the Art and Crafts Movement, but it was in fact healthier, for he taught a fundamental attention to structure and put ornamental style into its secondary place.

Stevens represents the Italian taste in opposition to the Gothic in the Battle of Styles which raged in the fine arts as fiercely as in the architecture of the nineteenth century. His style of decoration was carried on by Stannus, Townroe and Sykes, but he left no direct successor in painting or sculpture. The younger group of artists of similar persuasion—Leighton, Poynter and Moore—were neo-Classics and aimed to go direct to Greek models for their paintings of Greek life and myth.

Leighton had reason to regret the unco-ordinated eclecticism of his training which was tinkered with in almost every artistic centre in Europe and even included a visit to Wiertz, the megalomaniac pictorial propagandist of Brussels. His most profitable time was spent from 1850 till 1852 with Steinle at Frankfurt. Steinle was a follower of the original Nazarenes, and his somewhat limited art was at least genuinely imbued with the sincerity and noble aspirations of those monastically-minded men. To this phase belong Leighton's two celebrated early drawings 'The Lemon Tree' and 'A Venetian Well Head'. These inevitably won Ruskin's enthusiastic approval, but more resemble scientific dissections of their subject than documents of sensibility.

In spite of an apparent ease of execution Leighton's paintings were not facile or slap-dash. His method was invariably to make a drawing of every figure in his picture in the nude, then a drapery study of the same pose, which he pinned by his easel. Often he would also make wax models of the figures in his works—a practice which explains the sureness of his first full-size sculpture 'An Athlete Struggling with a Python', cast when he was forty-seven years old.

The essential factor of his style was that each individual figure should be in as balanced a pose as a Greek sculpture, and that the whole composition should form an agreeable unity. But this did not always preclude the intrusion of violent dramatic gesture; and in 'The Resurrection', as in 'The Sea gave up its Dead', he conceived an amazed and blinded human being with powerful effect (Plate 58).

Leighton commands our respect not only as an artist but also as a man of wide culture and catholic taste. His advocacy led to the completion of the abandoned Wellington Monument by Alfred Stevens, and his drawings are reproduced in the first number of the Yellow Book along with those of Aubrey Beardsley.

Poynter is remembered today, if at all, as the chief of the 'Marble painters', those makers of much-copied and highly finished scenes in which Grecian maidens repose languorously before the bath or in sight of the Mediterranean. It is hardly fair that his whole work should be judged by a formula which he developed late in life and under pressure of many official duties. Some of his more arduous works, such as 'Atalanta's Race' and 'Israel in Egypt', have become standard illustrations in children's encyclopaedias, and this gives them a far-reaching influence which they merit not only for their archaeological accuracy but also for their carefully realized sense of form and design. The impulse to paint subjects from Egyptian as well as Roman life doubtless came from Poynter's master Gleyre, who had his most intense imaginative experiences on the Nile. Poynter was a more sure and graceful draughtsman than Leighton and a stronger one than Moore. Whether he is drawing cherubs for the decorations of St Paul's, a musician playing on an ancient instrument (Plate 51), or figures stoning St Stephen, his touch is delicate and his sense of rhythm does not desert him. Such a master of academic drawing might have been expected to be an excellent teacher, but in this respect his term of office as first Slade Professor and subsequently as Director of Design at South Kensington is disappointing. His drawing books urge the students to make spiritless copies of the Raphael cartoons, of which he gives virtual tracings. His admiration for the French school led him to choose Legros as his successor in the Slade Professorship, but this did nothing to lift English art out of the trough of provincialism into which it was falling.

Albert Moore is if possible even more unfashionable at the moment than Leighton and Poynter. His friezes of Greek girls, into which a Japanese feeling enters at second remove, are closed worlds in which indolence is made delightful. A German critic wrote of them, 'It might be said that the old figures of Tanagra had received new life, were it not felt, at the same time, that these beings must have drunk a good deal of tea.' How exquisitely pretty his drawings could be, in the favourite neo-Classic medium of charcoal heightened with white on toned paper, is illustrated by Plate 50.

Both Leighton and Poynter designed a few illustrations of striking originality for Dalziel's Bible Gallery of 1881, but their designs for wood-engraving do not play a large part in their output. A number of admirable draughtsmen consolidated the renewed tradition of English illustration. Boyd Houghton combined consummate mastery with genuine Eastern atmosphere in his illustrations to the *Arabian Nights* and enraged the Americans by the caustic record of their civilization he sent back to the *Graphic* from the United States. Pinwell introduced a new sweetness into his closely observed scenes of country life. But the most admired of all, abroad as well as at home, was Charles Keene. His reputation has possibly been harmed rather than helped by the disposition to grant him exclusive praise, as though he alone among the English journalist draughtsmen of the nineteenth century merited the name of artist. Those we have already mentioned can successfully challenge this assumption. Keene was slow in coming to maturity; the designs he made in 1859 for *The Cloister and the Hearth* are graceless and unpleasing, and often when he drew from the model he could be as wooden as the student of a correspondence college. Yet when all this has been admitted he retains a very high place among our native draughtsmen through his free, later manner. On Leech's untimely death in 1865 Keene was asked to take his place on *Punch*, to record manners and customs, and particularly the humours of the middle and lower classes. It was at this juncture that Du Maurier was also engaged by *Punch* with instructions not to be too funny but to undertake the light and graceful business, to be the romantic tenor while Keene 'with his magnificent highly-trained basso, sang the comic songs'. It was a task for which there was a splendid reservoir of example in the foregoing hundred years of English graphic humour, reinforced by the situations of the English novel; and it developed in Keene an infectious streak of natural humour. He invented a great many of the jokes he illustrated, and the characters he depicted have the foibles he observed on his long walks in the streets of London. The broad line of his reed pen and his watered inks make a pleasing medium, and he has a natural eye for pattern which invests his drawings with an unstudied grace. Above all he had a wonderful feeling for light playing over a scene, putting the details in their subsidiary place and making the action immediately explicable and enjoyable to the eye (Plate 47 bottom).

No one could be more different from the robust, healthy, very English Keene than Aubrey Beardsley; in him the note of decadence which marks the close of the century asserts itself. Satanism, diabolism, the search for *le nouveau frisson*, had been in the air for some time; but with the partial exception of Sandys the manifestations of this frame of mind had so far been confined to literature in England. Swinburne had written hauntingly of the delights of flagellation and Lesbianism:

> *Ah that my lips were tuneless lips, but pressed*
> *To the bruised blossom of thy scourged white breast!*

and of

> *The shameless nameless love that makes*
> *Hell's iron gin.*

Walter Pater had been constrained to erase the conclusion, with its programme of aesthetic contemplation, from the second edition of his *Studies in the History of the Renaissance* because he 'conceived it might possibly mislead some of those young men into whose hands it might fall'. And when in 1891 in 'The Picture of Dorian Gray' Oscar Wilde proclaimed the New Hedonism—'The only way to get rid of a temptation is to yield to it', aiming to write a book where 'in exquisite raiment, and to the delicate sound of flutes, the sins of the world were passing' before the reader's eyes, all that the French had to contribute to the adulation of evil was naturalized here. It was a form of decadence only possible to a people who still believed in the reality of sin, and that particular religious gift was still very much alive.

Beardsley entered into this heritage as though he were born to be the illustrator of vice, perversion and subtle suggestion. His satanism was no pose, or the works it conjured forth would have lost their power as fully as the meretricious creations of Rops or von Stuck. Only Gustav Moreau bears any comparison with him as a draughtsman of decadence, and his bejewelled Byzantinism is nothing to the deeply intentioned evil of Beardsley's line. His published works were more venomous than the blatantly erotic drawings which were sold surreptitiously from the 'curious' cupboards of Smithers' bookshop. His dying cry of anguish 'I implore you to destroy all copies of Lysistrata and bad drawings.... By all that is holy all obscene drawings' can have availed him little at the Throne of Grace, for every mature drawing he made added something to an unbroken saga of the unholy. The poison is inoculated not by the incidentals only, the naked body, the bared breast, the powder puff, the slippers or the cane, but by the merging of these symbols into the distortions of natural proportions, the leering, androgynous faces, the insinuations of the design.

Satanism sprang from the ruins of the historical curiosity of the Romantics. The programme Dorian Gray set himself in emulation of Des Esseintes was 'to realize in the nineteenth century all the passions and modes of thought that belonged to every age except his own and to sum up, as it were, in himself the various moods through which the world spirit had ever passed, living for their mere artificiality those renunciations that men have unwisely called virtue, as much as those natural rebellions that wise men still call sin'. With the same resolve Beardsley set out to appropriate from literature and art the materials for an unparalleled mode of expression. Besides the books he did illustrate —*The Morte d'Arthur*, *Salome*, *The Rape of the Lock*, *Mademoiselle de Maupin*, *Volpone*, itself a wide-ranging group—he had planned to illustrate *Les Liaisons Dangereuses* and the *Comedy of the Rheingold*. His library included the works of Voltaire, Balzac, Racine, the Prose Works of Richard Wagner, and as the most prized volume of all, the *Lives of the Saints*. This catholicity of outlook is reflected in his graphic style. Upon a medievalism derived from Burne-Jones followed rapidly, during the eight years of his working life, the influence of Japanese prints, Greek vase painting, the eighteenth-century vignettists, and Mantegna. Because from the outset he had been taught to work with the recently perfected photo-mechanical processes in view, his line drawings were perfectly adapted to reproduction. The play of sensibility, change of pressure or tint and approximation of outline are deliberately excluded to subserve that end, and the result justified the means. However much erasure or correction we may feel has been effaced from the completed drawing, the fundamental certitude of the vertiginous line in, for example, 'Siegfried' (Plate 53) justifies Whistler in calling Beardsley the last of the writing masters.

Whistler himself almost defies classification in a national school; born in America he was trained in Paris and settled in England. By temperament and through the paintings of his twenties he belongs to l'École de Paris—in 1864 he was painted by Fantin-Latour by the side of Baudelaire, Manet and Braquemond in his 'Homage to Delacroix'—and yet his watercolours carry on the purest traditions of the English school. It is a matter of debate how far his skilful use of flat decorative surfaces was a whole-hearted tribute to Japanese examples and how far it was a device to cover up a known weakness in modelling. Whistler himself regretted not having paid closer attention to the precepts of Ingres when he was a student, and Sickert came perilously close to the truth when he asked Whistler how many of his pictures he had finished and how many he had left off working on. 'Young man, you are beginning to know too much,' was Whistler's reply. Gifted as he was in many ways, and handicapped in many, it was essential that he should know when to stop; and in his happiest works he has given proof of genius by realizing the precise point at which his sketch or painting has ceased to be unfinished and has become a unity. The design for a portrait of Mrs Louis Huth, his 'Arrangement in Black No. II' (Plate 42), is such a work. The curves of the silhouette, the relation of the head and bodice to the skirt, have the quality of the ceramic masterpieces Whistler admired, and the pose of the figure and the balance of whites and blacks are arranged with the delicate and almost feminine taste which was the strange counterpart of his bullying behaviour.

A gentler cosmopolitan of American descent, Sargent's childhood somewhat resembled Leighton's in its vacillation between the artistic centres of Italy and Germany. Before he too settled in London he had received his most formative instruction in Paris. Carolus-Duran, his teacher, was an academic with less taste than Gleyre (whom Whistler is said to have called a 'bourgeois Greek') but he had devised a precise method of teaching based on the principles of Hals and Velasquez, and the painstaking attention he gave to these studies was at the root of Sargent's dazzling technical facility. When he was twenty-five Henry James wrote of 'a talent which on the very threshold of its career has nothing more to learn'. The brilliant and fresh pencil portrait of Vernon Lee (Plate 55) is an early work made before that immense prowess had been blunted by too much popularity and too many fashionable portraits.

The German School

★

GERMANY remained, like England, for a long time untroubled by the revolutionary developments of painting in Paris. A spirit of naturalism, typified by Menzel and Leibl, was the prevailing frame of mind in the second half of the century, succeeding alike to the ascetic sincerity of the Nazarenes, to the romanticism of Runge and Caspar David Friedrich, and to the grandiose historical frescoes of Cornelius and his pupils. In mural painting and book illustration the German artists of the middle years of the century, Rethel, Retzsch and Menzel, taught much to the English; and in return the landscape painters of Germany learned from England, in particular Menzel from an exhibition of Constable's works which took place in Berlin in 1839.

Unlike France with its one artistic centre in Paris, and England with its main artistic centre in London, German painting, like its academic life, has revolved round a number of equally important provincial centres. By migration from one to the other the student could choose between the historical painting of Munich, the genre of Düsseldorf, the naturalism of Berlin. But there were lonely spirits who could not find their spiritual needs in any of these centres; and they, obeying a deep-seated urge of the German artist's nature, turned south to Rome. The 'Deutsch-Römer', Feuerbach, von Marées, Böcklin, form a trilogy comparable in their choice of subject-matter with Leighton, Poynter and Moore, but their work has a higher intensity through the greater passion with which they seize hold of classical learning, and by their more introspective approach. They lived out the same desire for the South which in the eighteenth century had made Winckelmann the founder of neo-Classicism and which Thomas Mann restated for the twentieth century in *Death in Venice*.

Moritz von Schwind, who has made a forgotten contribution to religious art in Great Britain in his designs of the 'fifties for windows in Glasgow Cathedral, may be chosen from many claimants to illustrate the survival into the second half of the nineteenth century of the creative effort of the Nazarenes. This group, of whom Overbeck, Cornelius and Schnorr von Carolsfeld were leading members, sought by the saintliness of their lives no less than by the imitation of the Primitive Italian painters to infuse art with a new religious spirit. They declined on grounds of principle to dilute their

46

perception of the ideal by working from the model. Overbeck, from modesty, refused to work at all from the female form. The resulting hardness and incorporeality of their graphic style is melted into a livelier grace by Schwind, who was born in Vienna and had become a devoted member of Schubert's circle. His lightness of heart, which led him to illustrate legends and fairy tales, is reflected in the answer he gave when he was asked to instruct a titled amateur in drawing: 'It does not require a day for that, my dear Baron; I can tell you in three minutes how I do it, I can give you all the desired information at once. Here lies my paper—kindly remark it, I buy it of Bullinger, 6 Residenz Strasse; these are my pencils, A. W. Faber's, I get them from Andreas Kaut, 10 Kaufinger Strasse; from the same firm I have this india-rubber too, but I very seldom use it, so that I use this penknife all the more, to sharpen the pencils; it's from Tresch, 10 Dienersgasse, and very good value. Now, I have all these things lying together on the table, and a few thoughts in my head as well; then I sit down here and begin to draw. And now you know all that I can tell you.' This advice might profitably be considered by critics as well as artists, and there is a correspondingly disingenuous charm about his two glimpses of Biedermeier interiors (see pp. 48 and 49) which combine rusticity with a sense of domestic comfort.

Menzel, the son of the owner of a lithographic printing plant, was left fatherless at the age of seventeen and thereafter obliged to support his family by his drawings. The colossus of nineteenth-century German art, he painted in his youth atmospheric landscapes and interiors which reflect his understanding of Constable, and in his later life pictures of modern industrialism and scintillating scenes of Potsdam society such as the 'Ball Room' which Degas admired. His great contemporary reputation as an illustrator was founded on his drawings for Kugler's *History of Frederick the Great*, but, in spite of their astonishing fidelity to the spirit as well as the detail of the eighteenth century, these have lost the immense prestige they once had. Our interest is compelled instead by the pastels and drawings of contemporary life which he made in great quantity, whether as studies for his oil paintings or for the sheer spontaneous love of observing and drawing for its own sake. In them he deals with plain unvarnished reality, and imposes on it sweetness and style through his preoccupation with the play of light over people and things, and through the liveliness of his line. In his portrait of a young woman seated at a table he is tender and wistful (Plate 65), in the drawing of a girl's head, on the same sheet as two studies of a hand holding a pair of pince-nez (Plate 69), he combines strength of modelling and minuteness of detail with graphic energy.

Menzel's was a temperament which found it easy to do what lay at hand and which was not concerned to do battle for ideals beyond its range. Doubtless his glorification of Frederick the Great, and his subsequent rendering of the charming surface glitter of Imperial Germany reflect, in those fateful years of the 1848 revolution and the unification of Germany, a political choice; but it was the choice of inertia or lack of interest rather than deliberate conservatism. The later-born, more thoroughgoing naturalist Leibl did not come so easily to terms with society. He admired Courbet and went to

SCHWIND: Interior at Carlsbad

study in Paris, but was forced to return by the outbreak of the Franco-German war. Thereafter he lived the life of a Bavarian peasant, a gesture in which may be seen the working of the processes of thought that led Millet to Barbizon or drew Van Gogh to work in a hovel amid miners. In his village he painted and drew with a remarkable objectivity, introducing into his realistic interpretation of that remote life a sensuousness in the treatment of surfaces which recalls the seventeenth-century Flemish painters. His portrait of a peasant girl of Aibling (Plate 64) is truthful and unsentimental in mood, but discovers rich, still depths in the unforthcoming enigmatic personality; and the study of folded hands (Plate 72) recalls in the intensity of the artist's observation, if not in the rhythm of the draughtsmanship, the famous praying hands of Albrecht Dürer.

The *Sachlichkeit* of Leibl had a surprising rebirth amid the turbulent cultural movements of Germany after the first World War in the Neue Sachlichkeit of Beckmann, Dix and Grosz. The combination of Classical theme and *staffage* with a nostalgic

48

schwind: Interior with girl

Romantic mood which was the keynote of the Deutsch-Römer had no such vital sequel, although it was to such models that Hitlerite Germany tried to put back the clock. To the retrospective eye Böcklin, Feuerbach and von Marées form an obvious and coherent group: but they were not consciously linked together during their lifetimes and their similarities of outlook are due to the community of temperament which made them feel that residence in Italy was essential to the formation of their styles.

Although he is naturally placed with the German school Böcklin is a Swiss-born painter. He was born at Basle and studied in Düsseldorf, Antwerp, Brussels and Paris; but once he had set foot in Italy he could not shake off the fascination of the landscape, and returned there again and again. Part of classical belief was reincarnated in him, in his intuitive comprehension of the relationship between nature and life. It was natural to him to think of the Italian landscape as vitalized by nymphs and dryads; the figures in his pictures have the appearance of being the earth spirits of the fields and trees. By the operation of this instinct Böcklin was able in 'The Isles of the Dead' to give form in simple and direct symbolism to a myth which awakens echoes in the depths of every mind. His success in this instance was almost too complete, for the overt anecdotal content has destroyed its reputation with those critics who, seeing only the story, are blinded to the poetic truth it embodies in the legitimate terms of painting. The drawing reproduced in Plate 66 suffers from no such obviousness of content, but is a true marriage between the landscape and the spirits by which it is peopled in the animistic philosophy.

Feuerbach's father was a professor of philology and archaeology, and implanted in his son a knowledge and love of the classics. His student years led him on much the same itinerary as Böcklin, from Düsseldorf to Munich, Antwerp and Paris where he learned a classicizing art under Couture. But it was in Italy that he became convinced of the fundamental excellence of the classical ideals of beauty, which thereafter remained his standard, and as a result of which he conceived his monumental paintings, among them 'Plato's Symposium', The Battle of the Amazons', 'Medea'.

The large oil painting of 'Medea' stands in an interesting relationship to the drawing (Plate 62) which was found on a piece of blotting paper after the artist's death. In the completed painting Medea is already a fugitive from her faithless husband Jason; she is resting on the rocks while the boat is being pushed out to sea; the nurse is bending her head in grief but Medea is calm in appearance, clasping her two children to her in an excess of maternal tenderness. In the drawing, as in the next sequence of an animated cartoon, everything has changed from the slow sadness of parting to the horror of bloodshed; the sorceress, beside herself, is killing her children, the hooded figure has dropped to a more abandoned grief. Feuerbach held that an historical painting must express the whole content of a life, its future as well as its past, and he had meditated for five years, as he records in his *Vermächtnis*, on whether to show 'Medea before the deed, Medea after the deed, Medea in flight by night on the beach, Medea as a loving mother, as a murderous Fury, sleeping, waking, in remorse and pain'. A gesture in a stage performance of *Medea* had crystallized these possibilities into the composition he eventually carried out, but the drawing suggests that he either meditated a sequel to hang beside it, or had regretted not choosing the more expressive and self-explanatory action. Into this sketch are compressed the horror and fury of a barbaric legend; but the drawing of a putto crowned with laurel (Plate 70) embodies the charm which he was able so winningly to combine with sureness of hand and sculptural finish.

The reputation of Hans von Marées has undergone strange vicissitudes. Neglected in his lifetime, frustrated by his own diffidence and lack of opportunity, he became renowned after his death and then, just as a reaction might have been expected, he was adopted by the National Socialist regime as the mascot of a healthy art in opposition to the modern creative work, from Liebermann to Munch, from Picasso to Klee, which was expelled from the Third Reich. Even the earlier and less bizarre of these estimates was based on an incomplete theory of aesthetics, of the kind made familiar in England through the writings of Roger Fry. Marées was held to have been engaged solely upon research into spatial and formal relationships, and his figures to be the abstract symbols in a sort of pictorial syllogism. It is incontestable that his pictures and drawings have a high degree of architectonic organization, and that he abandoned naturalism for this more generalized approach. But the recognition of the meaning of the landscape and the figures is no less important in the work of Marées than in Cézanne, with whom he has often been compared. Less fantasy-ridden than Böcklin, less theatrical than Feuerbach, he too is a poet haunted by memories of the Golden Age. The drawing reproduced in Plate 63 does not merely represent five naked forms held together in the frozen ballet of a beautiful design; these are young men and women picking golden fruit in some enchanted Hesperides. It was Marées' calamity to be denied the large wall spaces he could have decorated with these haunting symbolist legends; and his drawings are therefore all the more important in enabling us to comprehend his ambition to combine monumentality with ultramundane truth.

The foundation of the Secession movement in Munich in 1894 was an event comparable with the formation of the New English Art Club in 1886 and marks the naturalization of French Impressionism on German soil. Liebermann accepted the presidency of the Berlin Secession group in 1898; the close of the century therefore virtually divides his career into two clean and conflicting halves. The cycle of influences in his style is a microcosm of two decades of development in France; for to the guidance of Courbet succeeded that of Millet and the Barbizon school (with that of the corresponding Dutch cult of Israels) represented in the two drawings reproduced here (Plates 67 and 68). Then in the 'nineties he abandoned themes of humble life for the analysis of light and nature under the spell of the Impressionists. In this way his development resembled Van Gogh's, but it was spread over a longer period and, just as Liebermann's social paintings were not so sombre, neither was the answering lyricism of his liberation so intense.

*   *   *

This survey of drawing in France, England and Germany in the second half of the nineteenth century comes to a close with the advent of Impressionism to Germany. In the decade following the end of the century Picasso, Braque and Léger, taking their cue from Cézanne, committed a far more violent assault on the traditional methods of design than any it had sustained hitherto. At the same time, the German School, following the lead of Van Gogh and Gauguin and under literary influences, founded Expressionism. But these more radical developments belong to a subsequent chapter of the history of drawing.

INDEX OF ARTISTS

WITH PLATE REFERENCES

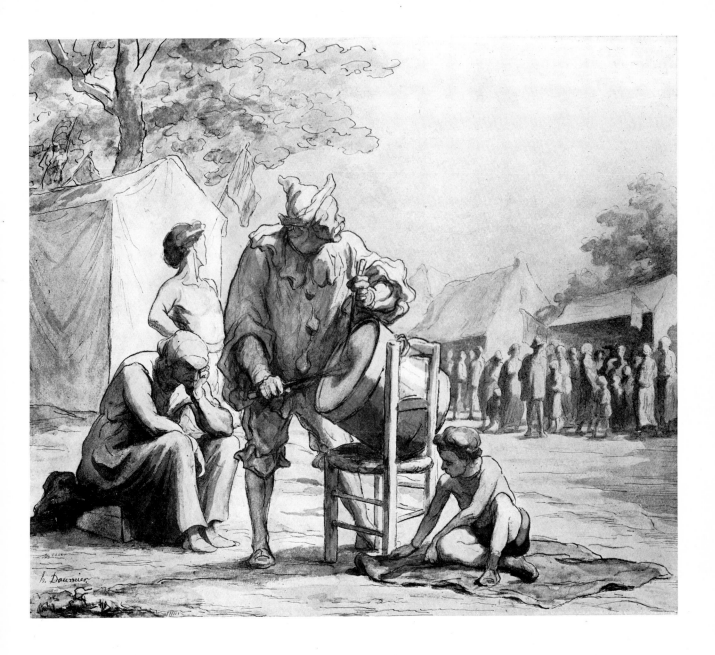

DAUMIER: The mountebank

D

DAUMIER: Allegory on the press

2

DAUMIER: Two barristers

BOUDIN: Ladies on the beach

MANET: Pertuiset the lion-hunter

3

4

MILLET: A Bretonne shepherdess

PISSARRO: A peasant girl

6

MANET: Study for 'Olympia'

DEGAS: Study for 'Les malheurs de la ville d'Orléans'

7

8

DEGAS: A horsewoman

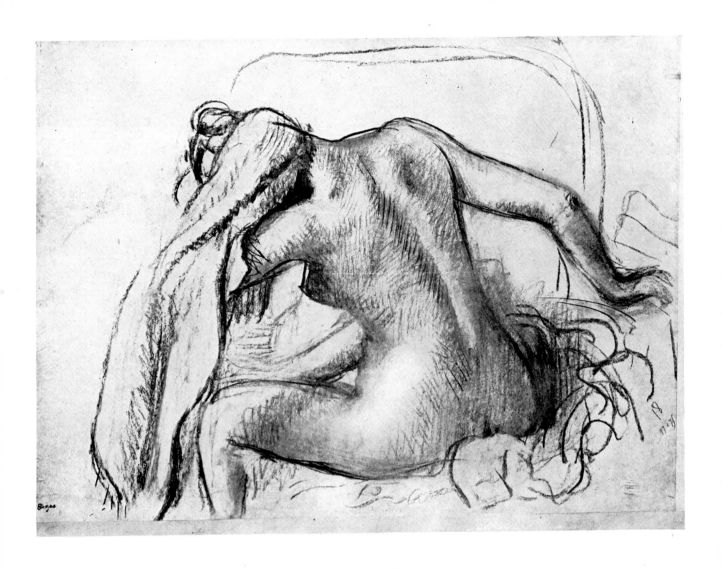

DEGAS: Woman drying herself

9

IO

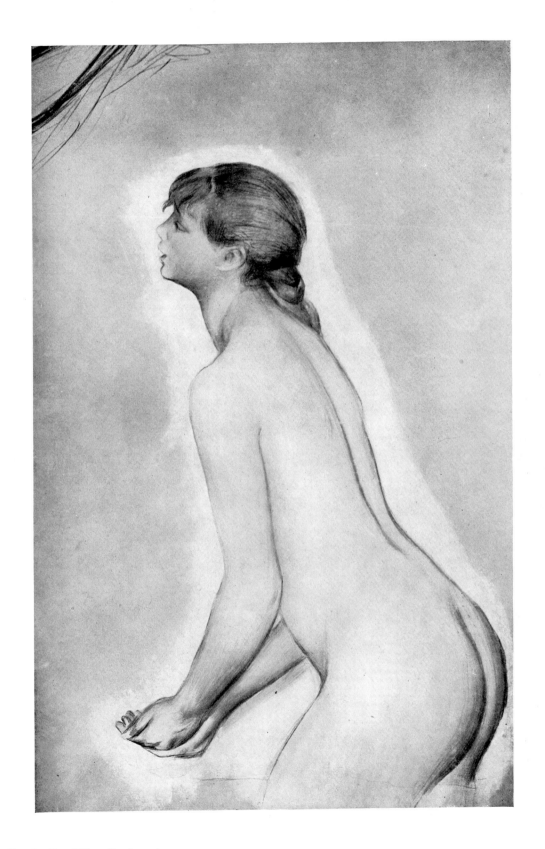

RENOIR: Study for 'The Bathers'

II

12

CÉZANNE: Study of male nude

13

14   TOULOUSE-LAUTREC: La Goulue and Valentin le Désossé

FORAIN: The plea

15

16   FANTIN-LATOUR: A woman sewing

SEURAT: Female nude

E

18   VAN GOGH: Cottages at Saintes-Maries-de-la-Mer

VAN GOGH: Stone seat in the hospital garden, St Rémy

19

20   CÉZANNE: The fisherman

CÉZANNE: Still life

21

22   DEGAS: Three dancers in tights

RENOIR: Little acrobats

23

24   BARGUE: The artist and his model

FORAIN: The artist and his model

25

26

RODIN: The embrace

RODIN: A female nude kneeling

29 Janvier. 66

28   FANTIN-LATOUR: Sugar-basin and tongs

RODIN: Seated female nude

30

TOULOUSE-LAUTREC: A woman lying in bed

LEGROS: Study of female nude

32   GUYS: Two women attended by men

SEURAT: At the *Concert Européen*

34   STEINLEN: Two masons watching a funeral

STEINLEN: A cat

36   GUYS: A carriage waiting outside a house

SEURAT: A group of people in front of a house

37

38

GAUGUIN: Tahitian men and women

40

GUYS: The graveyard scene in *Don Giovanni*

42

ROSSETTI: Miss Siddal standing by a window

43

44

MILLAIS: Girls in a meadow

45

MILLAIS: Study for the head of Ophelia

46

BURNE-JONES: Study for 'An Idyll'

ROSSETTI: Study for the head of the woman in 'Found'

KEENE: The nursery

47

HUGHES: Illustration to *Enoch Arden*

SANDYS: 'If'

G

49

50

MOORE: Two girls in classical dress

POYNTER: Study for a musician in 'The Queen of Sheba's visit to Solomon'   5I

BEARDSLEY: Prospectus for *The Yellow Book*

BEARDSLEY: Siegfried

53

54

SARGENT: Vernon Lee

56

STEVENS: Two studies of female nude

57

58

LEIGHTON: Two studies of female nude

59

60

BÖCKLIN: A faun whistling to a blackbird

61

FEUERBACH: Medea killing her children

MARÉES: Composition with five naked figures

63

64   LEIBL: A peasant girl from Aibling

MENZEL: A young woman sitting at a table

H

66

LIEBERMANN: A man digging potatoes

68

MENZEL: Studies of a young woman's head and right hand

69

70

MARÉES: Lovers bidding farewell

71

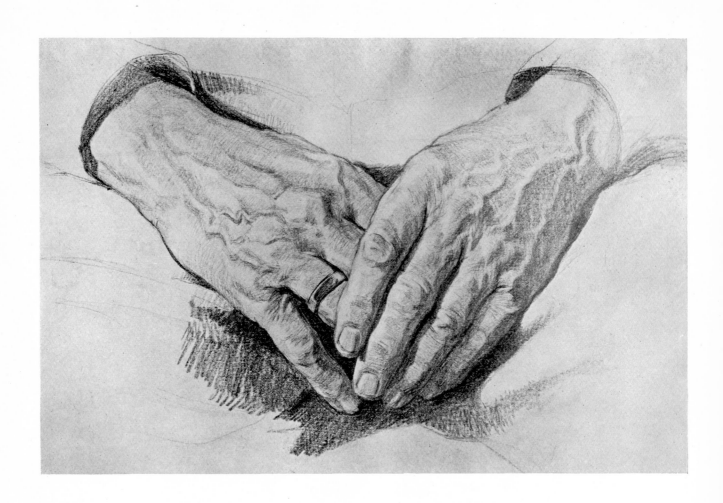

72